14 WEEK
BUCKET LIST

A SEASON OF COLLEGE FOOTBALL

ANTHONY WHITLOCK

This is a work of nonfiction. The events and experiences described are based on the author's memory and perspective. Some names and identifying details may have been changed to respect the privacy of individuals.

Edit by Michael Sandlin

Cover and Interior Formatting by KUHN Design Group | kuhndesigngroup.com

ISBN: 979-8-9996454-0-1 (paperback)
ISBN: 979-8-9996454-1-8 (eBook)

First Edition

Published by Anthony Whitlock

*This book is dedicated to my wife, Kim,
who has been my anchor and unwavering
support throughout the years. I love you.*

*To my daughters, Lauryn and Kennedy—you fulfill my
every dream of being a father. I love you. Be sweet!*

CONTENTS

FOREWORD

When I embarked on this journey, the only certainty was that the football games themselves would happen. While I knew most game times and dates, everything else remained delightfully undefined. My plan was simple: arrive in a new city on Friday, attend the game on Saturday, and return home on Sunday. What happened in between was largely unscripted, and therein lay much of the adventure's appeal.

This approach marked a significant departure from my natural tendencies. As someone who typically arrives at airports three hours early and meticulously plans every detail, embracing uncertainty was outside my comfort zone. Yet, this deviation from my usual planning habits became one of the journey's most rewarding aspects.

As someone with a reserved personality, perhaps the most dramatic shift in my behavior was my decision to approach strangers and share my story. My standard introduction became, "Hi, I'm Anthony from Austin. I'm doing a fourteen-week bucket list where I'm going to a different college game in a different city for the entire season." While this level of social initiative wasn't natural for me, it led to countless meaningful interactions.

The conversations often followed interesting patterns. Some people would carefully skirt around asking if I was terminally ill, the word "bucket list" triggering concerns about my health. Others would immediately question the financial aspects of my plan, to which I'd consistently respond, "Yes, it's expensive, but it's not going to take me to zero." Questions about my wife's support for this adventure were also common, allowing me to share that part of the story as well.

What emerged from these interactions was a remarkable discovery about college football culture. Regardless of political views, race, gender, or other potentially divisive factors, the spirit of college football created a uniquely welcoming environment. For those few hours on Saturday, all other distinctions melted away as people united in their love of the game.

The most unexpected and fulfilling aspect of the journey was its impact on others. Many people I met had never encountered someone actively pursuing a bucket list. My story often catalyzed conversations about their own dreams: whether it was visiting state parks, traveling to specific countries, or pursuing other personal goals. As I shared the story of my journey, people often felt inspired and would introduce me to their friends, hoping it might ignite the same motivation in them to pursue their own "someday" dreams.

This journey has left me with vivid memories from all fourteen weeks, exactly as I'd hoped. While I've experienced wonderful family vacations and daily blessings throughout my life, this adventure was unique in its personal nature. Every decision, every moment, was filtered solely through my own perspective, creating a distinct set of experiences that were entirely my own.

INTRODUCTION

I n 2024 at the age of fifty-three, I decided to embark on a bucket list journey: not because of illness or impending mortality, but because I wanted to create something memorable that was solely mine. Throughout life, we often focus on doing things for family and others, but this adventure would be different. This was about pursuing a personal passion that had been simmering since childhood: college football.

Growing up in Houston in the 1970s, our connection to the world came through just six channels: ABC, CBS, NBC, two local affiliates, and PBS. It's hard for people today to imagine, but these stations actually ended their broadcast day, typically around midnight, with the national anthem playing over a waving American flag, followed by static and that distinctive white noise that would fill both the screen and room. There was no 24/7 ESPN, no NFL Network, no endless stream of sports talk shows or instant highlights on your phone. When the game was over, it was over—no postgame analysis, no social media reactions, no constant updates about what players were saying in the locker room.

Football existed in specific time slots: college games on Saturday, NFL on Sunday, and Monday Night Football to start the work week. Outside of these windows, if you wanted football news, you had to wait for the morning paper or the evening newscast's three-minute sports segment. There were no instant replays to watch on your tablet, no YouTube highlights to relive great moments, and no fantasy football apps to check. The newspaper's sports section became almost sacred; you'd read every word because that's all you had until the next day's edition arrived.

This scarcity made every football broadcast special. When Howard Cosell's voice announced the start of *Monday Night Football*, it was an event. You couldn't pause it, rewind it, or stream it later. You either saw it live or you missed it. Pregame shows weren't day-long affairs with dozens of analysts: they were simple presentations giving you the basic information you needed to enjoy the game. The limited access meant you appreciated what you got. You savored every moment of coverage because you knew once that static hit the screen, football was done for the day.

Today's constant stream of sports content and instant access to information would seem like science fiction to my 1970s self. Back then, you couldn't google a player's stats or pull up their highlights on demand. You couldn't tweet about bad calls or join online discussions about coaching decisions. The game existed in real time, and then it lived on in memory and conversation until the next broadcast window opened. In many ways, this limitation made football more special—it wasn't background noise or constant entertainment. It was appointment viewing, something you planned for and looked forward to, making each game feel like a genuine event rather than just another option in an endless stream of content.

My team loyalties were split between two franchises. As a hometown fan, I followed the Houston Oilers, but I also found myself drawn to the Pittsburgh Steelers. Their colors captivated me, and I loved watching the Terrible Towel being waved on TV. Franco Harris became my Steelers hero, while Earl Campbell embodied everything exciting about the Oilers. In those days, team merchandise wasn't what it is today. I'll never forget one of my prized possessions: a makeshift Steelers jersey that was really just a black T-shirt my parents had customized at a shop in Sharpstown Mall. They pressed "Steelers" on the front and Franco Harris's number on the back. It wasn't anything like today's official jerseys, but to me, it was everything.

On the college side, I didn't initially have a dedicated team, but I found myself increasingly drawn to the University of Michigan. Their distinctive winged helmet design caught my eye, and their fight song became embedded in my memory. In the late 70s and early 80s, I followed receiver Anthony Carter—partly because we shared the same name. Michigan played in Houston's Bluebonnet Bowl during that period, and while I didn't attend the game, their presence in my city deepened my connection to the team.

My personal football "career" was brief and unofficial. I'll never forget one particular incident involved my attempt to re-create a goal-line stand, using our living room couch as the line of scrimmage. The glass sliding door a couple feet behind the couch proved an unforgiving opponent when I attempted to dive over the couch, resulting in me earning not a touchdown but butterfly stitches on my forehead and an ass-whipping. At River Oaks elementary school, we created our own version of football during recess. Using my prized lunch box—decorated with NFL team helmets—and its thermos, we'd play a makeshift game. We'd throw the thermos high into the air, and whoever caught it would run toward our designated end zone while others attempted to tackle them. It wasn't exactly regulation football, but those playground games captured the pure joy of the sport.

At Pershing Middle School, my dreams of playing organized football were cut short in the beginning of my eighth-grade year when I broke my right ring finger during a breakdancing incident—specifically, attempting the crab walk. By the time I reached Bellaire High School, football had become something to watch rather than play. Friday nights at Butler Stadium, where most Houston Independent School District games were held, became more about social interaction than serious football fandom. Football games, particularly homecoming, provided the backdrop for community gathering, though not with the same intensity as today's Friday Night Lights culture.

In 1989, I arrived at the University of Texas at Austin, stepping into a college football environment vastly different from what it is today. I didn't have a student sports pass that would have granted me access to all the games. While we were part of the Southwest Conference, UT football wasn't the powerhouse operation it is now: there weren't massive television contracts, state-of-the-art facilities, or the kind of funding that drives today's program.

The stadium itself tells the story of how different things were. Memorial Stadium held just under 80,000 people then, with a track circling the artificial turf field. Getting into games wasn't particularly difficult. (I'll admit I snuck into a few.) The atmosphere around game days was nothing like the spectacle it is now. Tailgating? I had no concept of what that even meant. The closest I came to tailgating culture was watching others do it years later. It's almost impossible to imagine now, but I've never even attended a Texas-OU game at the Cotton Bowl, despite it being the program's signature rivalry.

Most of my friend group didn't have cars, so traveling to Dallas for the game simply wasn't part of our college experience.

Football games were just something to do in the fall, not the all-consuming events they've become. My crew and I were more focused on attending classes, playing dominoes, hitting up video games, and going to parties. Sure, we'd go to some games, but it wasn't this must-attend ritual where you planned your entire semester around home games. I did maintain enough interest to return for a few games after graduation, including the memorable day when Ricky Williams broke the rushing record. But during my actual student years, football was more background noise than main event.

This wasn't unique to me; it reflected the different role college football played in campus life back then. We didn't have constant updates about recruiting, spring practice wasn't a media event, and you didn't have position battles being debated on social media. The game day experience itself was simpler: you showed up, watched the game, and went about your day. There was no ESPN College Game-Day atmosphere, no massive entertainment complex built around each kickoff. Looking back, it feels almost quaint compared to the modern spectacle college football has become, with its luxury boxes, massive video boards, and endless media coverage.

Well into my "adulting" years (as the millennials call it now), I reflect on a time around 2010, when I had an experience involving three coworkers that offered me a window into different stages of life I hadn't yet reached. Keith would talk about sending his daughters to college, describing the reality of facing each semester's college fee bills that needed to be paid all at once. At the time, with my own daughters still young, these conversations felt distant but served as an early warning of what I would eventually face. Billy, an older colleague, would mention concepts that weren't even on my radar in my forties: Medicare, Medicaid, and retirement planning. While I couldn't fully relate then, his insights now prove valuable as I navigate my fifties and contemplate my own retirement years. Then there was Storm whose woodworking passion showed me what retirement could look like. Here was someone who had every tool imaginable and found genuine joy in building things, not to sell or profit, but purely for the satisfaction of creation, which was his aspirational retirement thing to do. Unlike Storm with his woodworking, I didn't have a hobby that I could envision carrying into my retirement years. I didn't want to force myself into something that wasn't authentic to my interests, like buying tools just to have a hobby. What I did have was a genuine love for football, particularly college football, with its rich traditions, passionate fan bases, and unique game day experiences.

The timing aligned perfectly with several major life milestones. With financial support from my wife and me, Lauryn, my oldest daughter, graduated from college debt-free. Kennedy, my youngest, was progressing through her college years, and I could clearly see the path to covering her remaining educational costs. Meanwhile, the end of our mortgage was finally within reach. Having these major financial hurdles either behind me or well under control created a window of opportunity for something I'd dreamed about but had previously set aside while focusing on family responsibilities.

These major financial milestones, combined with good health, created a window of opportunity. However, the decision was also shaped by sobering realities. Both my parents had passed—my mom in 2002 and my dad in 2017—and I'd lost various friends and colleagues to accidents, cancer, and other ailments. These losses served as powerful reminders that tomorrow isn't guaranteed.

My wife's Uncle Gary, who retired from Motorola in his late fifties, became another influential figure. His consistent advice to "work to live, not live to work" and his successful transition to retirement in North Carolina provided a model for balanced life planning. These various influences led me to contemplate what would bring me genuine satisfaction in my later years.

The original bucket list started as a dream of attending every *Monday Night Football* game in a season. However, as I thought more deeply about it, I realized college football offered something more compelling. Instead of some climate-controlled NFL domes, I wanted the authenticity of outdoor college stadiums. Rather than facing a potentially mediocre Monday night matchup, which is only one choice per week, I could choose the most intriguing college games each week. The energy of college football—with its bands, traditions, and campus atmospheres—called to me more than the professional game.

The transition from dream to reality began taking shape during a Fourth of July pool party at my friend Greg's house in 2024. Initial conversations with friends followed the familiar pattern of sayings such as "someday, going to, should do, wanna do, thinking about and wouldn't it be cool if", but I was determined to move beyond hypothetical discussions.

As we guys hung out, our conversation flowed naturally through the usual topics: family updates, work situations, career moves, and catching up on our kids. Some of the guys had their kids playing high school football and were discussing their travels to different schools showing interest in their kids. It was one of those comfortable conversations where everyone's sharing life updates and future plans. I can't pinpoint exactly how the bucket list came up again, but when it did, I shared my dream of doing this college football journey to attend a game every week for the entire season. That concept was met with a sense of excitement among the guys as it was definitely a unique idea that went beyond planning a guys' trip. That's when Mitch jumped in with something that would help shape the entire adventure. "Man, if you end up doing that," he said, "why don't you come to J-State? I've been going to the Jackson State homecoming for the last few years. Make sure you put that on the agenda."

The enthusiasm in that pool discussion energized me. I returned home and opened up my iPad to begin mapping out the beginning phases of the journey. I used GoodNotes app my daughter had recommended. My approach was methodical: start writing out line items for each of the fourteen weeks and then begin to think about what's needed for each week. Obviously, first I would figure out what games are scheduled each week and where they'll be played. Once a game looks promising, I would need to secure lodging with flexible cancellation policies, in case some unknown situation with planning would arise. I would then solidify renting a car, as this also had flexibility with its cancellation policies, then move forward with airfare. The game ticket would be last. This strategy provided maximum flexibility while minimizing financial risk.

Inclusion of family and friends was not a primary goal. I was crystal clear from the beginning about the nature of this journey. This was fundamentally *my* bucket list, designed around *my* preferences and schedule. My approach was straightforward: "This is where I'm going to be," not "When can everyone make it?" I wasn't going to delay or adjust my planning waiting for others to check their calendars or coordinate schedules. If someone could join, great, but the trips would proceed exactly as I planned them, with or without others.

A major consideration in this solo-first approach was the simple logistics of traveling alone. Moving as a party of one offers tremendous flexibility: from booking flights to getting a seat at a crowded restaurant to securing single-game tickets. There's flexibility to solo travel and planning that disappears the moment you add even one more person to the equation. I wanted the freedom to move forward and get whatever suited me, whether it's the city I'm most interested in exploring, a particular seat that was available on a plane, or the opportunity to snag a single game ticket in a prime section without worrying about finding multiple seats together.

Most importantly, traveling alone meant complete autonomy over how I experienced each game day. If I wanted to arrive on campus eight to ten hours before kickoff just to soak in the atmosphere, I could do that. If something interesting in the city caught my eye and I wanted to explore it before or after the game, I didn't need to consult anyone else. Even something as simple as finding a quiet spot to people-watch and let time pass—these moments of solitude and observation were part of how I wanted to experience this journey. I didn't want to navigate different preferences, accommodate various comfort levels, or coordinate multiple schedules.

The schedule planning required careful consideration of multiple factors. Using ESPN's schedules as a foundation, I mapped out weeks one through fourteen, balancing several key considerations. Cost management led me to include some drivable Texas games among the flight-required destinations. I prioritized venues I hadn't visited before, with Michigan's Big House and Ohio State's Horseshoe high on my list. The allure of possibly seeing Appalachian State and the beauty of West Virginia called to me, though logistics would require careful planning. While I loved venues like LSU's Tiger Stadium, I opted to focus on new experiences rather than revisiting familiar grounds.

I laid out all individual fourteen weeks with options and filtered down the games based on several criteria until I had a final verdict. The planning wasn't done in one sitting rather over several weeks as some factors continued to play out.

Travel logistics became a crucial planning element. Based in Austin, Texas, which isn't a major airline hub, I needed to carefully coordinate flights to ensure I could depart Fridays and return by Sunday afternoon or early evening. Weather considerations also influenced the schedule: northern venues would need to be visited earlier in the season to avoid potential snow and extreme cold that might affect later games.

My wife Kim's support proved pivotal in transforming this dream from idle conversation into reality. When I first shared the bucket list concept with her, rather than questioning the time or expense involved, she immediately encouraged me to pursue it. "You've worked hard your entire life," she said. "You've got our family in a good financial position. I think you should go do it." That simple endorsement was powerful, but it was her next action that truly set everything in motion. After sharing with her the game that was highest on my list to attend, she offered to buy my Week Two ticket to the Texas-Michigan game at the Big House as my upcoming August birthday present.

This wasn't just a gift. It was her way of calling my bluff, of saying, "I believe in this dream enough to invest in it." With that gesture, she eliminated any possibility for me keeping this in the "someday" category. Her support went beyond the initial encouragement. She understood that this wasn't just about watching football games but rather about me creating something meaningful for myself after years of focusing on family obligations.

What made her support even more meaningful was that she didn't try to turn this into a series of couple's trips or family outings. She recognized that this was my personal journey, something I needed to experience in my own way.

Once she bought that ticket, the journey became real. I couldn't just talk about it anymore. I had to start making concrete plans. Her belief in this dream, coupled with her practical support in helping it take flight, transformed the bucket list from an interesting idea into an actual itinerary waiting to be fulfilled.

#7 NOTRE DAME AT #20 TEXAS A&M

The 2024 college football season opened with a prime-time clash between #7 Notre Dame and #20 Texas A&M at Kyle Field in College Station, TX. This Saturday evening game, kickoff on August 31st at 6 p.m., would mark the beginning of my fourteen-week journey. The choice stemmed from a personal connection: Leonard, the son of our neighborhood friends, had earned a scholarship to play for Notre Dame. College Station's two-hour driving distance from Austin offered a perfect starting point, allowing me to ease into the bucket list adventure without the complexities of air travel.

The planning crystallized through a conversation with my friend Greg, whose son played high school football. With Texas high school games scheduled for Friday nights, his Saturday was open. I was direct about my approach. On August 10th, I secured two tickets through SeatGeek in section 347, row five, seats 28 and 29, knowing we'd be in the third tier of Kyle Field's impressive three-level, 100,000-plus capacity stadium. While the end zone location wasn't prime seating, it would offer a perfect vantage point to absorb the full stadium atmosphere.

The group unexpectedly expanded on August 22nd when DKirk and Mitch reached out with surprising news: they'd managed to secure tickets in the exact same section and row, just a few seats down from us. While we wouldn't be sitting directly together, sharing the same section meant we could experience the game as a group while maintaining our individual viewing perspectives.

Although I come from a University of Texas background, I have always held a deep respect for Texas A&M's football culture. The rivalry between these two schools is one of the most storied in college football, stretching back over a century. Known as the "Lone Star Showdown," the fierce competition between the Longhorns and the Aggies has gone beyond sports, representing a clash of cultures, traditions, and even school pride, with each fan base as passionate as the other.

Texas A&M's passionate fan base, often playfully dubbed a "cult" for their remarkable dedication and the famous "12th Man" tradition, was something I was eager to experience firsthand. With each team only having eleven guys on the field, the fanbase is like an additional twelfth player, always standing, always yelling, always backing the A&M team no matter what. From Midnight Yell Practice—where thousands gather the night before games to rehearse coordinated chants—to the Corps of Cadets leading the team onto the field, and fans standing the entire game in support, Texas A&M's game day traditions felt more like a ritual than a routine.

The fact that this would be the first primetime matchup of the 2024 season, complete with ESPN's College GameDay broadcast from campus, only amplified my anticipation.

Before DKirk's arrival, I felt compelled to document the start of this journey. That Saturday morning, I recorded a short video outlining what was about to unfold: not just for this game, but for the entire fourteen-week adventure ahead. Standing in my driveway, I captured my thoughts about embarking on this bucket list, explaining how Notre Dame versus Texas A&M would serve as the launching point for what I hoped would become an unforgettable series of experiences. There was something powerful about verbalizing these plans, making them feel more real and concrete than when they were just ideas in my head.

DKirk picked me up at 12:30 p.m., right on schedule, and what could have been a routine drive turned into an unexpected highlight of the day. With Houston native DKirk's playlist setting the vibe—filled with screwed and chopped tracks, a signature Houston sound where songs are slowed way down and cut up for a hypnotic, laidback feel—we spent the drive laughing and lying all the way to College Station. Our conversation flowed easily between anticipation for the game ahead and random stories from our past, creating that particular kind of camaraderie that only road trips can inspire.

We'd made prior contact with Leonard's family about their tailgate spot, and while we weren't entirely sure what to expect, we made a quick stop at a liquor store to pick up some spirits and non-alcoholic beverages, along with snacks as our contribution. The mood in the car was electric: a mixture of excitement for the game ahead and the simple pleasure of friends embarking on an adventure together.

As we approached College Station just after 3 p.m., the streets were already filling with game day traffic. That's when the reality of a college football Saturday really hit us: cars with Texas A&M flags waving, people walking in their Aggie maroon and white, and the distant view of Kyle Field rising above the landscape. Without a predetermined parking plan, we navigated the side streets near the stadium, eventually finding a makeshift dirt lot where we paid $20 to park. It wasn't ideal, but it beat being stuck in traffic, so we took the opportunity and moved on, ready to immerse ourselves in the game day experience.

We made our way to campus around 3:30 p.m., navigating through a sea of maroon and white to find Leonard's family's tailgate spot. What we discovered was more than just a typical game day setup: it was a full-scale celebration where Notre Dame and A&M families had created their own little community. Multiple tents provided shelter from the Texas sun, with lawn chairs scattered about and several TVs showing the afternoon's college football games. The aroma of Texas barbecue filled the air: brisket smoking, hamburgers sizzling on grills, and an impressive spread of food that spoke to true Texas hospitality.

During these pregame hours, I found myself in several engaging conversations about my fourteen-week bucket list journey. It started when a group of Notre Dame parents asked what brought me to College Station. Their reactions shifted to genuine interest as I explained my plan to attend fourteen different college football games across the country. "Week One of Fourteen," I'd say, watching their expressions shift from surprise to enthusiasm. Despite not having any other stories to tell yet, the concept alone sparked excitement and countless questions about where I was headed next, how I planned it all, and what inspired such an undertaking.

One Notre Dame dad, particularly intrigued, shared stories of his own college football travels following their son's team, but admitted he'd never considered attempting something as ambitious as fourteen consecutive weekends. "You've got to document this," he insisted, echoing the sentiment I'd felt that morning when recording my pre-trip video. These conversations reinforced that this journey might be about more than just watching football; it could inspire others to pursue their own bucket list dreams.

The tailgate atmosphere was perfectly balanced between celebration and relaxation. Leonard's family had welcomed us completely, insisting we help ourselves to everything from the chopped beef sandwiches to the full bar they'd set up. Despite the temperature hovering in the 90s, the excitement of game day kept everyone's spirits high. We moved between groups, sharing stories and soaking in the distinct pregame traditions of both fan bases.

What struck me most about the tailgate scene was how effortlessly it dissolved the usual barriers between strangers. Here were Notre Dame families from across the country and Texas A&M locals, people who might never cross paths in ordinary life, sharing food, drinks, and stories as if they'd known each other for years. Our differences—whether geographical, political, or cultural—seemed to evaporate in the warmth of Texas hospitality and shared anticipation for the evening's game. I watched as northern accents mixed with southern drawls, as people from different walks of life swapped football stories and family tales. The beauty of it lay in its simplicity: no one had to try to make this work; it just did. The common ground of college football created a natural foundation for connection. Whether you were helping yourself to brisket from someone else's grill or offering your cooler of drinks to passing strangers, there was an unspoken understanding that we were all part of something bigger than our individual allegiances. This wasn't forced inclusion or manufactured camaraderie; it was genuine human connection happening organically around a shared passion. As I explained my fourteen-week journey to curious listeners, I realized that this might be one of the most valuable aspects of the entire bucket list: witnessing how college football creates these temporary communities where differences don't divide but rather add to the richness of the experience.

Around 6 p.m., as we began our walk to Kyle Field, we stumbled upon another welcoming community: the Soul of Aggieland tailgate. This group of African American alumni and current students had created their own vibrant celebration, with music and energy that drew us in immediately. Though our visit was brief, maybe fifteen minutes, their warmth and enthusiasm left a lasting impression. They insisted we come back for future A&M home games, demonstrating the kind of inclusivity that makes college football special.

The walk to the stadium was a full-on immersion into the spectacle of an A&M game day—Cadets in crisp uniforms marching in formation, vendors waving white 12th Man towels in the air, and a steady stream of maroon-clad fans all flowing toward Kyle Field. With every step, the buzz of anticipation grew, and I found myself trading stories with strangers who were just as fired up. One older gentleman walking beside me asked where I was from, and when I told him I was on a mission to attend fourteen college football games in fourteen weeks, his eyes lit up.

"Man, that's awesome," he said, grinning. "You're going to see how we do it here at A&M. Just wait until you see us do the Aggie War Hymn, the whole stadium will be swaying side-to-side."

Conversations like that didn't just pass the time—they added layers of perspective to the journey I was about to begin. This was more than just a Saturday in College Station—it was the first chapter of something much bigger.

As we approached Kyle Field, the sheer scale of the stadium became apparent. We entered about fifteen minutes before kickoff; the energy intensified as we climbed to our seats in section 347. The view from the third tier was impressive, offering a panoramic perspective of the field and the sea of maroon and white filling the stands.

I had deliberately chosen to dress neutrally for this game, a strategy I was already considering for future solo trips. While Greg confidently sported his Notre Dame hat, his 6'4" frame deterring any serious harassment, I was more cautious. I'd already overheard a few Aggie fans tossing playful jabs at some of the more obviously dressed visitors, like one guy shouting, "Hey Irish, you get lost on your way to South Bend?" with a grin and thumbs-up. While the A&M crowd seemed generally respectful, I was aware of how "liquid courage" could sometimes alter fan behavior.

The pregame festivities kicked into high gear, showcasing the full might of A&M's traditions. The Corps of Cadets took center stage, their crisp movements and precision adding a military air to the proceedings. As they performed the "Star-Spangled Banner," a perfectly timed military helicopter flyover sent a wave of excitement through the crowd. The massive JumboTron lit up with the phrase "moment where legends are born," followed by a montage of A&M's greatest plays, celebrating the legacy of the 12th Man.

The stadium erupted as the A&M band and flag bearers lined the end zone. On one side, individual maroon letters spelled out "TEXAS A&M," while on the other, flags waved to form "AGGIES." The anticipation reached its peak as Kanye West's "Power" thundered through the speakers. White smoke billowed from the center tunnel, and the A&M team burst onto the field to a deafening roar, met by a sea of waving white towels. The contrast was stark when Notre Dame entered through the corner tunnel of the same endzone, greeted by a chorus of boos as their own flag bearers ran

onto the field with their individual lettered flags proudly displaying "IRISH."

Throughout this spectacle, I found myself alternating between
soaking in the atmosphere and sharing observations with Greg beside
me. DKirk and Mitch, though seated a bit further down our row,
would occasionally catch our eyes, exchanging nods and grins of
appreciation for the unfolding scene.

As kickoff approached, Greg and I engaged in conversation with
fans behind us who discussed the intricacies of A&M's famous "yell
practice." They explained how these sessions, held Friday night before
each home game, ensured that tens of thousands of fans could move
and chant in perfect unison. It was a testament to the dedication of
the A&M faithful, and I made a mental note to compare this level
of coordination with what I'd see at future games.

As the teams took the field for kickoff, I felt a surge of excitement: not just for this game but for the journey I was embarking
upon. Week One was about to officially begin, and with it, a season
of discovery, adventure, and the pure joy of college football in all its
varied glory across the nation.

The game unfolded as a defensive struggle, with both teams trading field goals throughout the first half. From our end zone vantage
point, we had a perfect view of several crucial plays that kept the
score deadlocked at 6-6 heading into halftime. Though DKirk and
Mitch were several seats away, we developed a system of nonverbal
communication: raised fists for defensive stops, arms outstretched
for close calls, and knowing glances when Leonard took the field for
his first collegiate snaps on defensive special teams kickoff coverage.

During the game's quieter moments, I found myself noticing small
details that added to the experience. I was particularly intrigued by

the staff member who walked out during timeouts with a sign showing the time remaining. I couldn't resist texting my wife a photo, joking about "finding my retirement job." The bands provided constant entertainment during breaks, while the Corps of Cadets' precise marching in their traditional leather boots added to the pageantry.

The electricity in Kyle Field never wavered. Every defensive stand brought the crowd to its feet, the synchronized swaying and chanting creating a visual spectacle as impressive as the game itself. Without any words displayed on the JumboTron, decades of tradition showed as alumni and current students moved as one, their voices merging in perfect unison through each cheer. This wasn't just a football game; it was a choreographed display of community and tradition.

The halftime show perfectly embodied A&M's military heritage, where the Corps of Cadets and band executing precise, regimented formations with almost mechanical precision. While other schools might opt for playful routines or upbeat music, this performance felt more like a military parade than typical college halftime entertainment. The rhythmic sound of the drums and watching the leather boots and traditional military music created an atmosphere more reminiscent of a service academy than college football. While it might have lacked the lighthearted fun typical of halftime shows, it was authentic to A&M.

Only Notre Dame could produce points in the third quarter with a running play that went for a touchdown. As the third quarter came to a close, the stadium buzzed with anticipation—not just for the final fifteen minutes of football, but for something else entirely. That's when the sound of the Fightin' Texas Aggie Band erupted from the stands with brass booming, and the drums rolling with military precision. At first, it felt like the opening to a movie—intense, grand, and full of buildup. The fans behind us leaned forward and said, "This is the War Hymn – Our Fight Song."

That name instantly clicked. This was what the guy referenced earlier during my walk to the stadium. Now I knew exactly what he meant. It wasn't just a song—it was a ritual. A declaration. A moment where tradition, pride, and pageantry collided. The energy shifted—not just in volume, but in unity. Thousands of Aggies suddenly locked arms and began swaying aggressively back and forth, causing the entire upper deck to visibly shake.

A breakthrough finally came in the fourth quarter for A&M when they scored their first touchdown, and the stadium erupted. As the cheers echoed through Kyle Field, I witnessed an Aggie tradition I'd only heard about: couples—young and old—turning to each other and sharing celebratory kisses. But the celebration didn't last long. Notre Dame answered with focus and fire, rattling off ten unanswered points to close out the game with a 23–13 win.

What impressed me most was how the A&M faithful maintained their incredible energy even as victory slipped away. The "12th Man" tradition remained in full force until the final whistle: no early departures, no waning enthusiasm. As a University of Texas graduate, I had to acknowledge that this display of unwavering support was something special.

After the game, we stayed in our seats for about thirty minutes, letting the crowds thin while reflecting on the experience. All four of us regrouped, sharing our observations about the 12th Man traditions and the overall atmosphere. Before leaving, I noticed several discarded souvenir cups, popcorn containers, and white towels. Something compelled me to gather these items as mementos—physical reminders of this memorable evening.

The thirty-minute walk back to our car provided time for further discussion, and we decided to extend the evening with a stop at a restaurant on the drive home. Over dinner, the conversation naturally turned to what lay ahead; the guys were curious about how other venues and fan bases would compare to what we'd just experienced. But I found myself resistant to thinking in terms of comparisons. This journey wasn't about ranking experiences; it was about collecting unique memories at each stop.

Week One had exceeded expectations in every way. The combination of personal connection through the guys joining me, an opportunity to see Leonard play, the intensity of A&M's traditions, and the quality of the game itself had set a high bar. But more importantly, it had validated the entire concept of this bucket list adventure. As we finished our meal and headed home, my mind was already turning to Week Two and Michigan's Big House, knowing each subsequent Saturday would bring its own distinctive character to this unfolding story.

#3 TEXAS AT #10 MICHIGAN

My planning for Week Two began on July 15 when I booked my Airbnb in Ferndale, Michigan. I chose this location for its proximity to the Detroit airport and its manageable 50-minute, 50-mile drive to Ann Arbor. This decision was influenced by my anticipation of heavy traffic for such a big game and a desire to avoid staying in Ann Arbor.

I was on a business trip in New York earlier in the week and traveled directly to Detroit Friday before the game. Suspecting there would be a large Longhorn fan base traveling to and from Austin, I decided to stay through Monday to avoid heavy Sunday airline, airport traffic. This decision worked out perfectly when I realized the Detroit Lions were hosting the Los Angeles Rams for the first Sunday Night Football game of the NFL season, providing an unexpected bonus to my football-filled weekend.

My wife surprised me for my August 14th birthday with a single game ticket for the Texas vs. Michigan game in Ann Arbor. The excitement of finally seeing the Big House and hearing Michigan's fight song "Hail to the Victors" in person had me on another level of excitement.

I arrived in Ferndale early Friday afternoon, around 3 p.m., after flying into Detroit and picking up my rental car. Opting for a low-key evening, I went to the grocery store, bought salmon, and prepared a meal at the Airbnb, making enough for leftovers on Saturday. That evening, I downloaded YouTube TV to watch sports, as the Airbnb lacked cable channels.

Saturday morning, I woke at 5 a.m., ready to embark on my game day adventure. Following my new ritual, I recorded a video describing the weekend ahead and my excitement for the day's festivities. By 5:30 a.m., I was on the road, GPS set for Michigan Stadium.

Arriving in Ann Arbor around 6:45 a.m., I found myself near the stadium, surrounded by cars lining up for designated parking lots. Opting for a nearby lot, I was met with an $80 parking fee, *ouch*. However, when the young attendant's credit card reader failed, he accepted my offer of $15 cash—a stroke of luck that left me with prime parking close to the stadium.

For this game, I chose to dress neutrally. Despite being a Texas alum and Longhorn fan, I was wary of wearing team colors while attending alone. With Michigan as the reigning national champions, Texas ranked #3, Michigan #10, and ESPN College GameDay in town, I decided to play it safe and blend in.

As dawn broke, the parking lot slowly filled with early tailgaters. With a noon kickoff, the scene was dominated by breakfast foods, fruits, and juices rather than the typical beer and heavy fare. Michigan fans set up tents adorned with team logos, while a noticeable contingent of Texas fans established their presence.

As the early morning light began to fill the parking lot, I noticed a lively group directly across from where I had parked. Their tailgate setup was impressive. It spanned three parking spots and was covered in a mix of Texas and Michigan pride. Burnt orange and maize and blue flags waived above tents, coolers were decked out in team logos, and folding chairs, jerseys and even the tablecloths reflected a blend of Longhorn and Wolverine spirit. The sight of rival colors coexisting piqued my interest, and I felt a mix of excitement and curiosity, wondering how fans of two opposing teams could come together in such harmony. At 7:50 a.m., I decided to walk over and introduce myself.

Approaching the group, I opened with, "Hi, I'm Anthony from Austin, and I'm doing a fourteen-week bucket list trip where I'm going to a different college game in a different city for the entire season." I recall as I was saying this, there was almost a sense of "I wonder who this guy is and what he wants." But that first impression quickly turned into a welcoming reaction that was immediate and warm. Their genuine curiosity about my adventure was evident as they peppered me with questions about Week One and eagerly inquired about my plans for Week Three and beyond.

This crew, a blend of Texas and Michigan fans who had traveled together for the game, welcomed me into their tailgate without hesitation. They offered me an impressive array of breakfast fare: plump strawberries, a variety of cheeses, juicy blackberries, crisp crackers, and other assorted morning treats. The warmth of their hospitality matched the warmth of the apple cider in my hands.

As we chatted, I found myself sharing details about the Texas A&M game from the previous week and my upcoming plans for Week Three: the LSU vs. South Carolina matchup. Their interest in my journey and willingness to include a stranger in their pregame festivities set a wonderful tone for the day. This impromptu ten-minute interaction reinforced the communal spirit of college football that I was discovering on this bucket list adventure.

As I departed from this group, we wished each other well for today's game—they also wished me safe travels for the upcoming season of games. Continuing my walk toward the stadium, I encountered another group of Longhorn faithful, immediately noticeable by their two magnificent Great Danes. One of the dogs was particularly eye-catching, sporting Longhorn horns on its head, both animals decked out in Texas gear. As I approached to admire the dogs and grab a photo, I shared my bucket list story with their owner.

"That's incredible," he responded, explaining how he makes it a point to attend one Longhorn road game each season, carefully selecting the most appealing matchup. The concept of committing to fourteen consecutive weeks of travel to different venues across the country left him amazed. "I thought I was dedicated doing one road game a year," he laughed, "but fourteen straight weeks? That's next level." We discussed the logistics and planning involved, and he shared his own experiences of traveling to various college venues over the years. We discovered that our travel habits were quite similar. We both enjoyed arriving in the game city a day early and loved being at the tailgate venue hours before kickoff to soak in the excitement.

Before parting ways, they insisted I take one of their Longhorn cups filled with apple cider—my first souvenir of the day. This interaction reinforced how my bucket list journey resonated with other college football enthusiasts, even those who considered themselves serious fans. Their reaction validated the uniqueness of my undertaking while highlighting the camaraderie among college football travelers, regardless of the scale of their journeys.

The enthusiasm in his voice as he wished me luck on my remaining twelve weeks was genuine, and I could tell he was mentally filing away the idea for his own future adventures. These brief but meaningful exchanges were becoming an unexpected highlight of my journey, each one adding a personal connection to the broader experience of visiting these historic venues. Exiting the parking lot as I was making my way toward ESPN's College GameDay location, I unexpectedly encountered Fox's Big Noon Kickoff setup. Rather than bypassing it for my original destination, I decided to explore this competing broadcast, a decision that proved rewarding. The production had transformed their area into an engaging festival-like atmosphere, anchored by a picturesque GREETINGS FROM ANN ARBOR MICHIGAN banner that made for perfect photo opportunities. A particular highlight was getting up close to the national championship trophy, its gleaming presence drawing fans for photos and creating a tangible connection to college football's ultimate prize.

The environment was electric, largely due to a talented DJ who did more than just play music: he orchestrated the entire experience. He achieved a masterful balance by engaging the growing crowd while preparing them for the upcoming broadcast; he understood exactly how to generate the energy levels needed for television while keeping everyone entertained. Michigan and Texas flags waved prominently against the morning sky, creating a colorful backdrop that captured the magnitude of the biggest matchup of the early 2024 season.

Just when I thought I had experienced the full scope of their production, the DJ announced that Moneybagg Yo would be performing. This unexpected addition to the morning's festivities—a major hip-hop artist at a college football pregame show—exemplified how sports creates an intersection with other forms of entertainment. Around

8:38 a.m., Moneybagg Yo took the stage, and I stayed for one of his sets, enjoying this surprising fusion of hip-hop and college football culture. The performance added another layer to an already dynamic morning before I continued my journey toward the ESPN setup. Fox's production had set a high bar for game day entertainment, demonstrating how competition between networks ultimately benefits the fans with enhanced experiences.

The area around Michigan Stadium was a sea of maize and blue, with pockets of Longhorn orange. I captured photos with the Home of the 2023 Champions logo before reaching the packed ESPN tailgate area. Making my way to ESPN's GameDay setup, I found myself among a massive crowd of passionate fans who had staked out their spots hours earlier. While I couldn't get close enough to the main stage for a clear view of the broadcast team, the atmosphere was exactly what I'd seen on television countless Saturday mornings—only now I was experiencing it firsthand. The iconic Ol' Crimson flag from Washington State, a GameDay tradition that began in 2003, waved proudly among the sea of other team flags, signs, and banners. Its presence marked an incredible streak of over three hundred consecutive GameDay appearances. The flag has been at every show since October 18, 2003. What started as one passionate fan's effort to bring attention to Washington State has evolved into one of college football's most beloved traditions, with dedicated alumni and fans ensuring the flag's appearance week after week, regardless of GameDay's location. Its unwavering presence serves as a powerful symbol of college football's grassroots spirit and the extraordinary lengths fans will go to support their teams, even when their own school isn't in the spotlight.

The creativity of the student section was on full display through their signs. Clever jabs at Texas mixed with proud declarations of Michigan's prowess filled the air: witty wordplay, memes, and the kind of irreverent humor that only college students can come up with. Some signs poked fun at Texas's SEC move, others played on Michigan's defending champion status, each one adding to the carnival-like atmosphere. One fan's sign read EVERYTHING'S BIGGER IN TEXAS EXCEPT THEIR TROPHY CASE. Home Depot's presence was evident through their branded orange hard hats and work gloves being distributed throughout the crowd, adding splashes of construction orange to the sea of Michigan maize and blue.

From my vantage point, I could catch glimpses of the various broadcast stations set up around the main stage. The familiar faces of college football's most prominent voices filled the monitors scattered throughout the crowd: Kirk Herbstreit breaking down key matchups, Desmond Howard offering his Michigan-centric takes, Pat McAfee bringing his trademark energy, Nick Saban adding championship-level insight, and Rece Davis steering the conversation with ease. Off to the side, Lee Corso readied himself for his legendary headgear pick—the grand finale of the show where, with theatrical flair, he dons the mascot head of the team he believes will win. Their discussion flowed from deep game analysis to broader storylines across the sport, all building toward the historical weight of this Texas-Michigan clash.

While I might not have been close enough to see every detail of the broadcast in person, being part of this GameDay atmosphere—something I'd watched on television countless times—felt like stepping into a familiar scene. The energy of the crowd, the blend of analysis and entertainment from the broadcast team, and the overall spectacle of College GameDay in person exceeded what television could ever capture.

After navigating the crowded GameDay scene, nature called, and I faced the dreaded sight of endless lines at the porta potties. However, some quick observation revealed people slipping in and out of nearby buildings. Taking a chance, I discovered the University of Michigan's ice rink facility. Inside, it was mostly empty except for a Zamboni driver methodically cleaning the ice and a few others who'd made the same savvy restroom choice. This proved to be a brilliant alternative to the porta-potty lines, and the clean, indoor facilities were a welcome luxury on a busy game day.

Upon returning to the GameDay area, I came across ESPN's College GameDay tour bus, a rolling monument to the show's history and prominence in college football culture. The massive vehicle served as a perfect photo opportunity, its sides adorned with larger-than-life images of the show's personalities. Each panel of the bus told a story of college football's most iconic pregame show, and I took my time capturing photos from various angles. The bus itself was a testament to how GameDay had evolved from a simple pregame show to a cultural phenomenon that helps define college football Saturdays.

This unexpected find turned what could have been a mundane bathroom break into another memorable moment that day. Standing there, taking photos with the GameDay bus, I felt like I was documenting not just my journey, but my small part in the larger tradition of college football fandom.

Returning from my unexpectedly eventful break, I discovered a relatively uncrowded area next to an athletic track where ESPN had set up Pat McAfee's field goal challenge, where a randomly selected fan can win cash prizes by kicking a thirty-three yard field goal live on the telecast. They had erected goal posts and marked off thirty-three yards for what had become a beloved segment of the show. I positioned myself along the barrier separating the track from the spectator area, unknowingly finding the perfect spot for what was about to unfold.

Around 10:28 a.m., the production crew appeared with McAfee's signature oversized check to be awarded upon a successful student's kick. To my surprise, they asked the person next to me to hold the check for the upcoming segment. Seizing the moment, I placed my hand on the check, too, becoming part of the background staging for the television shot. The camera crew moved in to film us, and suddenly I was part of the GameDay production—an unexpected thrill for a longtime viewer of the show.

The selected student arrived with football in hand, and I had a chance to chat with him briefly before his attempt. "How did you get picked for this?" I asked. He explained it was a random drawing, and he'd had barely any time to prepare once his name was chosen. Despite his admission of having no real football background, he maintained a positive attitude about his upcoming moment in the spotlight.

The excitement amplified when Kirk Herbstreit made his way down to our area to watch the attempt. Before the kick, he graciously interacted with fans, including me. I managed to get a quick selfie with him, finding him to be friendly and engaging despite the hectic atmosphere. He offered me a fist bump and carried himself with the same natural charisma that comes across on television.

As for the kick itself? Well, it wasn't exactly highlight reel material. The student's attempt was nowhere near successful, sailing well wide and short of the target. But in the spirit of the moment, it hardly mattered. The entire experience—from holding the check to meeting the student to interacting with Herbstreit—had created another memorable chapter in my game day adventure, one that showed how being in the right place at the right time can lead to unexpected moments of joy.

As 11 a.m. approached, I made my way toward the Big House, feeling a surge of anticipation with each step. Entering the stadium, I was immediately struck by the sea of Michigan maize and blue slowly filling the vast bowl before me. The sheer scale of Michigan Stadium was awe-inspiring: a single-tier behemoth capable of holding over 107,000 fans, making it the largest college football stadium in the nation.

I found my seat Section 6, Row 13, Seat 42 what was designated as the visiting section, predominantly populated by fellow Longhorn fans, their burnt orange creating distinct pockets amid the sea of Michigan colors. Interestingly, even in this "away" section, there were sprinkles of Michigan supporters, adding to the electric atmosphere of this intersectional clash.

The unique design of the stadium became apparent as I settled into my spot. Despite being just thirteen rows from the field—close enough to see the players' expressions and hear the on-field chatter—I realized the concourse level was a considerable distance away, at the very top of the stadium. This design quirk meant that any trips to concessions or restrooms would require a significant trek up and down the expansive seating area.

As kickoff neared, the stadium came alive. Yellow pom-poms began to wave throughout the stands, creating a shimmering effect that rippled across the crowd. The single-tier design amplified the noise, with cheers and chants reverberating around the bowl in a way that made the already massive crowd feel even more imposing.

From my vantage point, I could appreciate the brilliant engineering that allowed this colossal venue to maintain an intimate feel.

Despite the vast number of seats, the pitch of the stands kept every fan close to the action. The lack of upper decks or overhangs meant an unobstructed view of the sky above, adding to the open, grand feel of the Big House.

As the stands filled to capacity, there was an increased surge of energy. The mix of anticipation, school pride, and the weight of the matchup's importance created an atmosphere that was both exhilarating and slightly overwhelming. Taking in the sights, sounds, and the sheer scale of Michigan Stadium, I realized I was about to experience college football in its purest, most grandiose form.

The pregame festivities at Michigan Stadium delivered everything I'd dreamed of and more. The Michigan Marching Band took the field, and when the first notes of "Hail to the Victors" filled the air, I felt goosebumps rise on my arms. This was the fight song I'd grown up watching on TV, the one that had first drawn me to Michigan football as a kid, and now I was hearing it performed live in the Big House. Through my binoculars, I watched intently as the band moved with precision, their formations crisp and their sound magnificent.

What struck me most was the unique configuration of the team entrance. Unlike most stadiums where teams emerge from the end zone, Michigan's tunnel was located at midfield. This setup created an even more dramatic entrance than I'd anticipated. The iconic "Go Blue M Club Supports You" banner was stretched across midfield in front of the tunnel opening, its maize and blue colors vibrant against the stadium backdrop. As "Hail to the Victors" reached its crescendo, the Michigan players burst from the tunnel, each one leaping to touch the banner as they emerged—a tradition that's been carried out for generations.

The moment was everything I'd hoped it would be. The coordinated timing of the band playing "Hail to the Victors," the crowd's roar with yellow pom-poms waving and the players' entrance created a symphony of college football tradition that gave me chills. This was more than just pregame entertainment; it was a piece of college football history playing out before my eyes, exactly as I'd imagined it for all these years.

As the entrance of the Michigan team concluded, the atmosphere quickly shifted. The Texas Longhorns, clad in their crisp white away jerseys, emerged from the tunnel onto the field. A cascade of boos rained down from the Michigan faithful, but these were quickly drowned out by the defiant strains of "Texas Fight," played by the traveling Longhorn band. The contrast was stark and thrilling: the sea of maize and blue momentarily disrupted by the proud burnt orange contingent, their fight song a bold declaration that they weren't intimidated by the Big House's hostile environment. This good mix of competing sounds and colors encapsulated the essence of a high-stakes SEC vs. Big 10 college football clash. *It's gametime!*

As the teams lined up for kickoff, the stadium buzzing with anticipation, I heard a voice cutting through the crowd noise. "Hey! Hey! I'm from Austin!" it called out repeatedly. The familiarity of the voice made me turn, and there, to my utter disbelief, stood my good friend Greg.

"Holy shit, dude!" I exclaimed, my voice filled with a mixture of shock and elation. "What are you doing here, bro?" The words tumbled out as I was overcome with excitement, unable to process this unexpected surprise.

Greg, grinning widely, explained that it had all been arranged as a surprise. My wife, Kim, had secured a second ticket, but Greg couldn't make it on Friday due to his son's football game. Instead, he'd caught the first flight out of Austin to Detroit that morning, drove straight to Ann Arbor, and made it just in time for kickoff.

This surprise addition to my game day experience added an incredible layer of joy to an already unforgettable day. As we embraced and quickly caught up, the energy of the moment—the impending kickoff, the roar of the crowd, and now the presence of a close friend—created a perfect storm of excitement. It was a reminder that while this journey was personal, sharing it with others could make it even more special.

The game itself quickly developed into a demonstration of Texas's superiority, with the Longhorns asserting their dominance from the opening quarters: it was a beatdown. The electric atmosphere that had filled the Big House during pregame festivities began to dissipate as Texas systematically dismantled the defending national champions. It didn't take long for the Longhorns to silence the majority of the fans in attendance—except for the Texas contingent growing louder with each successful play.

By halftime, with Texas holding a commanding 24-3 lead, the mood in the stadium had shifted dramatically. The sea of yellow pom-poms that had created such a vibrant spectacle early on now lay largely dormant. Michigan fans, who had entered the stadium riding the high of their 2023 national championship, sat in stunned silence as their team appeared completely outmatched by the more talented Longhorns.

Throughout the second half, Texas continued to control the game, ultimately securing a decisive 31-12 victory. The defending champions never mounted a serious threat to get back into the contest, and the steady stream of fans heading for the exits early in the fourth quarter told the story of Michigan's disappointing performance.

One of the most intriguing observations during the game came from the modern evolution of college football displayed on the video boards. QR codes flashed periodically, encouraging fans to contribute to players' Name, Image, and Likeness (NIL) deals: a fascinating glimpse into how the sport's economics had evolved. The sight of these digital payment portals in the Big House, one of college football's most historic venues, created an interesting mix of tradition and progress. While players getting paid was now commonplace (meaning *officially* legit), seeing it marketed so openly in a stadium that had witnessed over a century of amateur athletics was a stark reminder of how much the sport had changed.

As the game wound down and fans began filtering out of the Big House, Greg and I decided to linger, letting the crowd thin out. With Michigan's record attendance of 111,170 announced during the game, we knew trying to exit immediately would be chaotic. This pause gave us time to soak in the Longhorns' dominant victory while also allowing me to continue my emerging tradition of collecting game-day mementos.

I noticed numerous fans leaving behind their maize and blue souvenirs—perhaps out of disappointment from the loss, or simply typical postgame behavior. I gathered Michigan souvenir cups and yellow pom-poms, each item a tangible reminder of this historic venue and memorable day. The collecting of these items was becoming a ritual of my journey, each piece holding a story from these legendary venues.

About an hour after the final whistle, we found Greg's rental car then made our way back to mine before heading to Ferndale. Having Greg stay at my two-bedroom Airbnb was perfect: another part of my wife's well-orchestrated surprise. We decided to head into Detroit for dinner, choosing a restaurant near Ford Field, where I'd be watching the Lions game the next day. The evening was spent reliving the game's highlights, catching up as friends do, and watching other college football games at the restaurant. The combination of Texas's victory, the unexpected reunion with a good friend, and the anticipation of the next day's NFL game created a perfect football Saturday.

Sunday brought a relaxed morning as Greg departed early for his flight home. I spent the day catching up on work and watching NFL games before heading to Ford Field for the Lions-Rams Sunday Night Football matchup. While the NFL atmosphere differed from the college experience, the overtime thriller—with Detroit winning 26–20—was a perfect cap to an incredible football weekend.

Reflecting on the journey back to Austin mid-Monday morning, I was filled with excitement for the adventures to come, particularly the upcoming weekend in Columbia, South Carolina, for LSU vs. South Carolina. Week Two had exceeded all expectations, blending the thrill of iconic college football traditions with the unexpected joy of shared experiences and NFL action.

#16 LSU AT SOUTH CAROLINA

As I evaluated my plans for Week Three, I found myself weighing several attractive matchups: Colorado vs. Colorado State, Washington vs. Washington State, West Virginia vs. Pittsburgh, Georgia vs. Kentucky, Alabama vs. Wisconsin, and Texas A&M vs. Florida. However, LSU vs. South Carolina stood out, particularly given my personal connection: my oldest daughter was an LSU alum. I had never been to South Carolina and wanted to give this venue a shot. On July 19th, I committed to the game, booking my Airbnb, airfare, rental car, and game ticket.

While I didn't know any current players on either team, South Carolina represented new territory for me. After observing fan behavior during my first two weeks, I felt comfortable enough to wear home-team colors, already having a maroon shirt and planning to purchase a Gamecocks hat once I arrived.

I landed in Columbia, South Carolina, early afternoon on Friday, September 13th. After checking into my Airbnb, I made a quick trip to Walmart, where I found a Gamecocks hat at a considerable discount compared to campus prices. With my game day attire sorted, I decided to take advantage of the early arrival and explore the campus.

Reaching the University of South Carolina around 4:30 p.m., I immediately noticed something unusual: the stadium wasn't on campus. This sparked questions about student access to games, a detail I'd learn more about later. With an enrollment of around 56,000, the campus itself was stunning, with historic buildings and majestic trees creating a picturesque setting for my self-guided tour.

During my wanderings, I discovered a powerful piece of history: a statue commemorating Robert Anderson, Henry Monteith, and James Solomon, the first three African American students to enroll at South Carolina on September 11, 1963. The memorial served as a poignant reminder of the civil rights struggle in the South. I also encountered lighter touches of campus culture, including a bronze statue of their mascot, Cocky, perfect for photo opportunities.

After picking up a walking tour map from the welcome center, I explored various residential halls before ending at the Russell House University Union, which housed typical campus amenities like dining facilities and administrative offices. Around 6 p.m., I left campus for dinner at the Blue Marlin Restaurant in the downtown area, where I enjoyed a meal substantial enough to provide leftovers after game day.

My Airbnb's location in the West Columbia River District proved ideal, offering access to local breweries, restaurants, and a scenic riverwalk complete with bridges and an amphitheater. I spent the evening sampling local brews and watching Friday night football games on YouTube TV.

Saturday, September 14th began early, as usual. Before leaving the Airbnb, I recorded my now-traditional video diary, outlining the day ahead and my expectations for LSU versus South Carolina. I had debated taking an Uber to the stadium but ultimately decided to drive. My reasoning was simple: with a noon kickoff, I'd be done by late afternoon, and having my own car would give me the flexibility to leave when I wanted rather than dealing with surge pricing or long wait times for rides after the game.

I pulled out of the driveway at exactly 6 a.m., wanting to beat any traffic and secure a good parking spot. The drive to Williams-Brice Stadium took only about twenty minutes in the peaceful predawn hours. As I approached the stadium area, I quickly realized street parking wouldn't work given Columbia's layout. After some searching, I found a lot with an attendant who offered a spot for $40. While the price seemed reasonable, his assurance that my car would be safe and the short twenty-minute walk to the stadium made it worth it.

Rather than immediately heading toward the stadium, I decided to make the most of my early arrival. I settled into my car, pulled up YouTube TV on my phone, and caught up on highlights from Friday night's games while also watching the morning's college football previews and GameDay preshow coverage. This quiet time allowed me to ease into the day while staying comfortable in my car as a light drizzle fell outside.

Around 8:30 a.m., I headed toward the stadium under overcast skies with a light drizzle, grateful for my windbreaker. The atmosphere was already building for what promised to be a significant game: #16 LSU was in town to take on an unranked South Carolina team, and remarkably, ESPN's College GameDay had chosen Columbia as their broadcast location. This marked the third straight week GameDay had coincided with my bucket list journey, making me wonder if they were following me around.

Making my way through the stadium lots, I encountered the unique charm of a morning tailgate scene. While not as boisterous as evening games, these early risers brought their own special energy, with the aroma of breakfast foods replacing the typical afternoon barbecue. The light drizzle didn't dampen anyone's spirits; if anything, it seemed to create a more intimate atmosphere among the dedicated fans who'd braved the weather.

I came across several welcoming groups who had already set up their spreads. Following my now-familiar introduction ("Hi, I'm Anthony from Austin, and I'm doing a fourteen-week bucket list…"), I found myself immediately drawn into warm conversations. The tailgaters were eagerly fascinated by my journey, peppering me with questions about Texas A&M's 12th Man tradition and Michigan's Big House while offering me their morning specialties.

One group had an impressive breakfast setup with homemade biscuits and gravy, fresh fruit, and hot coffee—a welcome sight in the cool morning air. Another had created a full-on brunch spread with breakfast casseroles and mimosas. Each group I met was interested in how their tailgating compared to what I'd seen at other venues. When I explained to them that morning tailgates seemed to have their own unique vibe compared to evening ones, they nodded in agreement, proud of their breakfast-themed traditions.

The conversations flowed effortlessly, shifting between football talk and classic Southern hospitality. Over plates of brisket and breakfast tacos, a group of die-hard Gamecock fans proudly walked me through their game day rituals—everything from arriving before sunrise to always bringing the same lucky folding chairs. As they passed me a plate, they peppered me with questions about my upcoming stops—curious if I'd make it to SEC powerhouses like Georgia or experience the chaos of a night game at LSU. Their fascination in my journey, paired with their warmth and generosity, perfectly captured the spirit I was beginning to associate with college football Saturdays. Though I'd started the morning a stranger, I was quickly folded into the community—each interaction deepening my understanding of just how diverse, proud, and passionate these fan cultures truly are.

As the clock struck 10 a.m., the game day atmosphere shifted into high gear. I found myself gravitating toward the ESPN College GameDay setup. However, having experienced the GameDay frenzy before, I opted for a different vantage point this time. I discovered a perfect spot in a courtyard nestled between the GameDay broadcast area and the South Carolina Gamecocks Radio Network setup. This unique location offered me a multisensory game day experience.

From where I was, I could hear the energetic analysis from the Gamecocks Radio team, their voices filled with anticipation for the upcoming clash with LSU. Simultaneously, the familiar sounds of the GameDay broadcast provided a national context to the local excitement. Adding to this auditory tapestry was live music from nearby performers, creating a perfect blend of national hype and local flavor.

As I sat taking in the scene, the energy of GameDay slowly came to life around me. Vendors bustled about, setting up their stands with practiced rhythm—griddles clanking, coolers thudding, banners flapping in the breeze. The air was rich with the comforting aroma of fresh-brewed coffee, blending with the unmistakable scent of hot dogs beginning to sizzle on open grills. A faint sweetness from cinnamon rolls drifted through the crowd, layered with the occasional whiff of hickory woodsmoke from a nearby BBQ setup that hinted at what would be on the menu by mid-morning. Fans streamed by, their faces painted proudly in garnet and black, holding steaming styrofoam cups and balancing breakfast plates as they made their way toward the action. Many clutched handmade signs—clever, bold, or downright hilarious—eager to claim a few seconds of fame in front of the GameDay cameras. As LSU lost their Week One game to the USC Trojans, my favorite sign read IF LSU COULDN'T HANDLE A TRO-JAN JUST WAIT TILL THEY SEE OUR COCKS. The entire scene was a feast for the senses, buzzing with anticipation and steeped in tradition.

This moment of relative calm before the game day storm allowed me to appreciate South Carolina's football culture. I observed the mix of longtime fans in well-worn Gamecocks gear chatting with excited students experiencing their first big SEC matchup. The convergence of national media attention and deep-rooted local traditions unfolded before me, providing a unique perspective on how a game day in Columbia comes to life.

It was during this time that I truly appreciated my decision to arrive early. Before the full roar of the crowd and the blaring speakers took over, the stillness of the morning offered a rare glimpse behind the curtain of a college football Saturday. I watched as vendors methodically arranged their setups, tailgaters unfolded chairs with practiced ease, and stadium staff moved with quiet urgency to finalize preparations. Without the noise and bustle, I noticed the subtle things—how the stadium lights cast a soft glow over Williams-Brice Stadium, the rhythmic cadence of the marching band's warmup echoing in the distance, and the way longtime fans greeted one another like family. This quiet observation period allowed me to soak in the authenticity of the scene—unfiltered and unhurried—adding a new layer of appreciation and depth to my understanding of South Carolina's football culture.

Around 10:30, the energy around the stadium shifted as fans began to gather, eagerly awaiting the arrival of the South Carolina team. The anticipation broke into cheers as the Gamecocks, led by their marching band, made their way through the crowd. Players exchanged high-fives with fans, the excitement infectious as the team prepared to enter the stadium for final preparations.

As the crowd dispersed following the team's entrance, I decided it was time to make my way toward Williams-Brice Stadium. It was around 10:50 a.m. when I began my approach, giving myself plenty of time to soak in the rest of the pregame atmosphere. As I neared the stadium, something completely unexpected stopped me in my tracks—a row of bright, refurbished train cabooses lining the edge of the stadium's western perimeter. Known as the Cockaboose Railroad, these twenty-two retrofitted railcars aren't just eye-catching—they're luxury tailgating suites complete with full kitchens, air conditioning, and rooftop decks. Fans were gathered outside each one, grilling, laughing, and waving garnet flags from the elevated platforms. It was unlike anything I'd seen at any other campus—a blend of railroad nostalgia and high-end tailgating that added a uniquely South Carolina twist to the game day experience. The sight of these bold red cabooses, each proudly flying the Gamecock colors, instantly elevated the already electric scene outside Williams-Brice Stadium.

Although Cocky remains the beloved and official mascot of the South Carolina Gamecocks, the Cockaboose Railroad has taken on a personality of its own—an iconic fixture that feels just as woven into the fabric of the university's culture. Since its origin in 1990, when a local real estate developer purchased 22 cabooses and a stretch of unused track, the vibrant railcars have become a symbol of South Carolina's unique blend of tradition, pride, and tailgating spectacle.

With my ticket for section 14, row 3, seat 27 in hand, I entered the stadium, also known as "The Cockpit," just after 11:10 a.m. The morning's light rain had given way to breaking clouds, hints of sunshine beginning to peek through. As I made my way to my seat, I was struck by the layout of the stadium. The entrance I used offered an unusually close perspective of the field, allowing me to fully appreciate the venue's design. I ended up taking a few photos with the stadiums JumboTron as a backdrop that read "Williams Brice Stadium" with "The Cockpit" written underneath it. I looked around the façade of the stadium for what was likely retired players' numbers—the only names I recognized were Jadaveon Clowney and Sterling Sharpe. Williams-Brice stadium holds just shy of 80,000 seats as a two-tier stadium on its sides, with one endzone being a single level, and the endzone I was seated in was three tiered.

This configuration promised an electric atmosphere once the stands filled. As I settled into my seat, I couldn't help but feel a surge of excitement for the game ahead, knowing I had one of the best vantage points in the house for this SEC showdown.

Finding my seat, I realized I had lucked into an incredible location. I was just three rows up in the end zone, providing an intimate view of the action. In the section to my right, I could see the LSU band setting up, promising an up-close experience of their performances throughout the game. In front of me were the stadium's hedges lining the end zone, adding a touch of Southern charm to the field.

Taking my seat around 11:30 a.m., I found myself next to Deborah her daughter Dominik, both dressed proudly in LSU purple and gold. After exchanging initial pleasantries, I leaned in conspiratorially and shared my "secret"—despite being decked out in South Carolina gear, I was actually an LSU supporter. This revelation led to immediate laughter and connection as I explained that my daughter was an LSU alum. Dominik's face lit up, sharing that she too had graduated from LSU, creating an instant bond through our Tiger connections.

The conversation deepened as I shared my fourteen-week bucket list journey with them. Their initial curiosity turned to genuine excitement as they asked questions about the games I'd already seen and the adventures ahead. Deborah, who revealed she was planning to retire in April 2025, found resonance in my story. As Deborah spoke enthusiastically about her own upcoming plans, which included attending more LSU games with her daughter and visiting her son in Austin, Texas. Her eyes lit up with excitement as she vividly described her aspirations for retirement: from enjoying extended family time to embarking on vacation travels she'd long dreamed about. Our discussion evolved into a broader conversation about seizing opportunities to pursue what brings joy in life, whether that's following college football across the country or creating new family memories. We reflected on how easy it is to postpone our dreams in the rush of daily responsibilities, yet how vital it is to make space for what truly fulfills us.

Deborah also noted that watching me pursue my passion for college football had inspired her to be more intentional about her own joy-seeking journey. The energy in our conversation shifted as we all recognized that pursuing happiness isn't just about grand gestures: it's about consciously choosing experiences that light us up inside, strengthen our connections with loved ones, and create stories we'll cherish for years to come. Whether it's the roar of a stadium crowd, quiet moments with family, or the thrill of exploring new places, these are the threads that weave together a life well-lived.

As the section I was sitting in was mostly populated with LSU fans, and at one point during our conversation (and in good fun), a passing South Carolina fan said to me: "You're in the wrong section, come sit with us!" This only served to strengthen my new impromptu game day bond. We took several photos together, capturing the unlikely friendship of Tiger supporters in Gamecock territory. As the game progressed, I found myself dropping my neutrality, quietly celebrating LSU's successes with my new friends while trying not to be too obvious about it in the home team's stadium.

Deborah and Dominik proved to be perfect game day companions, their genuine warmth and shared love of LSU football making the experience even more memorable. Our conversation flowed naturally between game action, family stories, and future plans, demonstrating how college football has a unique way of bringing people together and creating lasting connections as we exchanged our contact information.

The pregame festivities brought unexpected surprises. I was familiar with Purdue's "train" tradition, which centers around the Boilermaker Special. This official mascot resembles a Victorian-era locomotive and roams the sidelines at games, symbolizing the school's engineering heritage. I had no idea South Carolina incorporated the Cockaboose Railroad beyond just tailgating but also as part of their game day culture.

From the opposite end of the football field, out from the endzone tunnel, came a red train and caboose. It stopped at the 30-yard line. The end of the caboose opened up to reveal Bree Hall and Raven Johnson, members of South Carolina's 2024 championship women's basketball team. They led the stadium in the traditional "Game-Cocks" cheer. One side of the stadium would cheer "Game," then the other side would respond with "Cocks." I noticed fans waving white towels, though not with the same intensity or sheer volume as the sea of maize and blue pom-poms I'd seen at Michigan the week before—highlighting how each stadium showcases its own distinctive traditions.

After Bree Hall and Raven Johnson energized the crowd, the stadium's attention shifted to the endzone. From the tunnel, white smoke began to emerge as the opening notes of "2001: A Space Odyssey" blasted through the speakers—an unmistakable cue for what was about to unfold. Used by South Carolina for decades, this electrifying musical track adds a sense of epic grandeur to their entrance, building anticipation with each booming note. As the South Carolina marching band formed two precise lines down the field, they created a dramatic corridor. Then, through the smoke and fanfare, the Gamecocks burst forth to thunderous applause, running between the band members who lined the path in a synchronized welcome. The moment, elevated by music, smoke, and crowd energy, was more than a team entrance—it was a theatrical declaration that kickoff had arrived at Williams-Brice Stadium.

The atmosphere quickly shifted as LSU prepared for their entrance from the opposite tunnel. In a spectacular display, flag bearers burst onto the field first, each carrying individual purple and gold flags spelling out T-I-G-E-R-S. They raced across the field in perfect formation, their flags whipping in the air, creating a dramatic visual backdrop for the team's entrance. The LSU players followed behind this wave of purple and gold, met by a combination of boos from the home crowd and passionate cheers from the substantial LSU contingent.

From my vantage point next to the LSU band, I had a perfect view of this choreographed spectacle. The contrast between the two entrances—South Carolina's smoke-filled, traditional run-through versus LSU's flag-bearing pageantry—highlighted how each program puts its own unique stamp on these pregame traditions. I watched in appreciation as both teams took the field, the energy in the stadium reaching fever pitch as kickoff approached.

Just as the energy in Williams-Brice Stadium seemed to reach its peak, the crowd was hit with one final sonic explosion. The Jumbo-Tron flickered, and the unmistakable instrumental of "Sandstorm" by Darude pulsed through the speakers—a tradition that since its 2009 debut has become synonymous with Gamecock football intensity.

Suddenly, Dawn Staley, the legendary head coach of South Carolina's women's basketball team and architect of three national championships, appeared onscreen. Her presence alone commanded attention, but it was her animated towel-waving that ignited the crowd. Fans throughout the stadium instantly mirrored her, whipping their white towels in unison to the beat, creating a swirling sea of movement. The ball hadn't even been teed up yet, but the Gamecocks faithful were now at full throttle. This wasn't just hype—it was a ritual that had evolved from a simple song selection to a defining game day tradition.

The game itself proved to be a thrilling back-and-forth affair, where South Carolina jumped out and showed dominance early by having the first 17 points unanswered before LSU scored with a ground attack. Each time LSU scored, the band would launch into their familiar touchdown traditions. I found myself fighting back smiles as they spelled out "T-I-G-E-R-S" through these scoring celebrations, trying to maintain my appearance as a South Carolina supporter while secretly reveling in these moments with Deborah and Dominik. South Carolina took a 24-16 score into the half while the second half now with LSU on offense heading toward the endzone I was sitting in, saw the Tigers battle back with a late fourth-quarter closing touchdown run to take their first lead of the game 36–33.

The Gamecocks were in a position to tie up the game, however, they missed the field goal in the last second, handing the Tigers the victory.

As the final seconds ticked off the clock, the LSU band delivered their victory celebration, including their rendition of Lil Wayne's "Right Above It." The song, which has become an LSU tradition, echoed through the stadium as purple and gold–clad fans celebrated. My attempted neutrality had ended, as Deborah, Dominik, and I celebrated LSU's success together. I found myself fully immersed in the joy of LSU's victory, the familiar sounds of the band providing the perfect soundtrack to another unforgettable bucket list experience. The combination of exciting football, the pulsing energy of the band, and the opportunity to share the experience with my new friends made this game particularly memorable.

Following LSU's victory, I maintained my now-established tradition of lingering in the stadium for about an hour after the final whistle, allowing the crowds to dissipate while collecting mementos of the day. I gathered a commemorative white towel that bore the date and matchup details, along with a souvenir cup—each item representing another chapter in my growing collection of game day memories.

Around 5:30 p.m., I made my way back through the thinning crowds to my car, the twenty-minute walk giving me time to reflect on another successful weekend of my bucket list journey. Back at the Airbnb by 6 p.m., I warmed up my leftover Blue Marlin Restaurant dinner before heading down to one of the River District's establishments I'd discovered on Friday night. Savage Craft Ale House provided a perfect setting to wind down, as I enjoyed a cold beer while watching the evening's college football games on the bar's TVs. The combination of good food, pleasant weather, and the satisfaction of another memorable game day created a perfect Saturday evening.

Back in Austin before noon on Sunday, I took time to appreciate another successful weekend of my bucket list journey. Columbia had offered a unique blend of Southern hospitality, college football tradition, and memorable moments. As I reflected on the experience, my excitement was already building for the following week's adventure: heading to Colorado with my oldest daughter Lauryn to watch Baylor take on the University of Colorado Buffaloes.

The South Carolina experience had added another distinctive chapter to my journey, each stadium and campus bringing its own character to the college football landscape. University of South Carolina's campus offered a moment of reflection—its historic walkways once marked by the struggle and courage of students during the early years of desegregation. That legacy of resilience now hums beneath a vibrant, unified student body. Williams-Brice Stadium stood out for the deeply embedded traditions that shape every moment of game day. From the Cockaboose to the shaking eruption of "Sandstorm," it felt like every fan, every beat, and every towel wave was part of a larger ritual of pride. Week Three had delivered everything I'd hoped for and more.

BAYLOR AT COLORADO

Week Four of my bucket list journey took me to Denver, Colorado, with plans to watch the Baylor Bears take on the Colorado Buffaloes in Boulder. Colorado moved from the Big 12 conference to join the Pac-12 in 2011. They returned to the Big 12 for the 2024 season, and this would be their first game back since re-joining the conference. This move was influenced by changes in conference alignments along with more favorable revenue opportunities. I booked everything on July 19, 2024: airfare, hotel, rental car, and game tickets, setting us up for what would become an unforgettable father-daughter weekend.

NFL Hall of Famer Deion "Primetime" Sanders left an indelible mark on professional football during his fourteen-season career. His exceptional versatility allowed him to excel as a cornerback, receiver, and return specialist, while his electrifying style and unshakeable confidence made him one of the sport's most memorable personalities. The "Primetime" nickname, given by a childhood friend, perfectly captured his flair for performing on the biggest stages, and has evolved to "Prime" and now "Coach Prime" in his current role.

As head coach at the University of Colorado, Sanders brought his trademark charisma and winning mentality to a struggling program, generating nationwide buzz for the team's transformation. Adding to the compelling narrative, he coaches alongside his talented sons – quarterback Shedeur and defensive back Shilo Sanders. This combination of family dynamics, Sanders' legendary status, and the program's resurgence made catching a game in Boulder an irresistible prospect.

On Friday, September 20th, we arrived in Denver mid-afternoon. I had flown in from Austin while my daughter Lauryn had come from Houston. Knowing Lauryn had just worked the night shift, and with Saturday's game scheduled for 6 p.m. mountain time, we planned for a low-key evening. We ventured into the Union Station area of downtown Denver around 5 p.m. for dinner. The downtown area was surprisingly quiet by 7 p.m., lacking the typical downtown energy you might expect. We took this as our cue to head back to the hotel and rest up for Saturday's main event.

Saturday morning kicked off just after 9 a.m. with breakfast in the hotel lobby. I wore my new *WE HERE* hoodie—more than just apparel, it was a statement echoing Coach Primes' bold declaration of presence and purpose at Colorado. Lauryn matched the energy, proudly repping a University of Colorado shirt. Together, we weren't just showing support for the team—we were part of the movement.

After a leisurely morning back at the hotel after running a few errands, we set out for the University of Colorado campus around 1 p.m. Lauryn and I made my pregame video at the hotel before we ventured off. We made the thirty-mile drive to Boulder for Colorado's homecoming weekend. The drive was scenic, with stunning mountain views and favorable weather: partly cloudy and comfortable temperatures. GPS was going to take us straight to Folsom Field.

As we got close to the stadium, we found parking easily in one of the garages and began exploring the campus. To our surprise, the campus was unusually quiet for a homecoming weekend. Lauryn, having attended LSU, noted the stark contrast to the electric SEC gameday atmosphere she was used to.

As we explored the campus, we found ourselves frequently pausing to take in the stunning backdrop of the mountains creating a framework for the university's architecture. The combination of well-maintained red brick buildings, mature trees, and majestic Rocky Mountains rising in the background created a breathtaking setting that made us wonder aloud how inspiring it must be for nearly forty thousand students to wake up to such views every day. Despite the quiet pregame atmosphere, the natural beauty of Boulder's campus was undeniable, offering a unique blend of academic dignity and outdoor majesty that set it apart from any other university setting I'd visited on my journey so far.

In 2024, music legends and entrepreneurs Dr. Dre and Snoop Dogg launched their premium gin-based cocktail, Gin & Juice, and held a bold and immersive pop-up marketing experience just outside the stadium on Colorado Avenue. The setup resembled a modern travel house—complete with white stairs leading into a sleek, branded structure that blended hip-hop with upscale cocktail culture.

Inside the house, visitors were greeted by a full-sized white refrigerator stocked with multiple flavors of the Gin & Juice cocktails. One wall featured a high-resolution digital mural of a classic low-rider Chevy Impala, with "Gin & Juice by Dre and Snoop" glowing above the vehicle in retro-style script.

Outside, the activation continued with lounge chairs, umbrella-covered high-top tables, and sofas draped in branded throw pillows.

T-shirts, koozies, and other Gin & Juice merchandise were given away, creating a casual but buzz-worthy retail vibe. Best of all, the pop-up bar served free samples of the cocktail, inviting guests to sip and chill in the laid-back atmosphere.

Around 1:30 p.m., we stumbled upon the setup and were instantly pulled in by the energy and detail. Front and center was a striking replica of a 1964 Chevy Impala on working hydraulics, catching every eye. Lauryn jumped at the chance to climb into the lowrider for a quick photo shoot while I hopped on a nearby custom low-rider bicycle, striking poses as she snapped away. We laughed, posed, and soaked up the uniquely Dre and Snoop experience that turned a simple product launch into a full-on cultural moment.

We settled into the lounge area, sampling different flavors while watching other fans interact with the Impala and lowrider bike. The whole scene felt surreal: enjoying Snoop and Dre's branded beverages in the shadow of the Rockies, on a college campus no less. It was these kinds of unexpected moments that made the bucket list journey special.

After about forty-five minutes of enjoying the atmosphere, taking photos, and relaxing in the lounge area, we reluctantly decided to continue our campus exploration. The Gin & Juice setup had provided the perfect father-daughter bonding experience, combining Lauryn's appreciation for good photo opportunities with my love for discovering unique aspects of each gameday environment. It was the kind of unplanned encounter that turned a quiet afternoon into a memorable moment we'd talk about long after the game was over.

Around 2:30 p.m., we encountered two fathers from Pennsylvania whose daughters attended Colorado. As we exchanged pleasantries, I shared my bucket list journey story. Their eyes widened as I detailed my weekly adventures across different college football venues. One of the fathers, a Penn State alum, immediately drew comparisons between the atmospheres. "This is nothing like a Saturday in Happy Valley," he remarked, but quickly added how fascinating it was to witness Colorado's transformation under Deion Sanders.

Our conversation deepened as we discussed how Colorado's gameday culture differed from traditional football powerhouses. The Penn State dad described the stark contrast between the sea of white at a Penn State game and the more relaxed, almost laid-back vibe in Boulder. Yet we all agreed there was an undeniable buzz in the air: not from decades of tradition, but from the fresh energy Coach Prime had injected into the program.

The other father mentioned how his daughter had described the dramatic shift in campus energy since Coach Deion Sanders took over the football program. What was once a low-profile team and afterthought of campus life had transformed into the heartbeat of student culture. Folsom Field had gone from half-empty stands to sellout crowds. National media outlets were now regular visitors, and Boulder—once overlooked in major football conversations—had become a center of attention. Students who previously had little interest in the team were now lining up for tickets, wearing CU gear, and following recruiting news. It was more than just football—it was a cultural reset, and the energy on campus reflected it.

This impromptu meeting reinforced one of my favorite aspects of the bucket list journey: how college football created connections between strangers, allowing us to share perspectives on the sport's evolving culture.

At 3 p.m., the official Fan Festival opened, but the atmosphere fell noticeably short of the high-energy environments I'd experienced at other venues. While the space was well-organized, the energy felt more like a casual community gathering than a major college football pregame celebration. The music lacked the pulsing excitement typically associated with gameday festivities, playing at a volume more suited for background ambiance than rallying a crowd.

We explored the festival area, eventually finding a local food truck that offered some excellent catfish and fries. While enjoying our meal, we observed how the crowd moved through the space—relaxed and unhurried, a stark contrast to the frenetic energy I'd witnessed at Texas A&M or Michigan. The festival had all the expected components—food vendors, merchandise tents, and activities—but seemed to operate at a different tempo, perhaps reflecting Colorado's more laid-back culture.

The setup appeared proportional to Folsom Field's smaller capacity, but even accounting for scale, the energy level seemed unnaturally subdued. However, this more relaxed atmosphere had its own charm, allowing for easier movement and more casual interactions. As Lauryn noted, comparing it to her LSU experiences, this was definitely a different interpretation of gameday culture—not better or worse, just distinctly Colorado.

Despite the lower-key environment, we found ourselves enjoying the authenticity of the experience. This wasn't a school trying to replicate SEC-style gameday chaos; it was Colorado doing game day their own way, even as the program underwent its high-profile transformation under Coach Prime.

Around 4 p.m., the atmosphere suddenly shifted as word spread that the team buses were arriving. The previously relaxed crowd quickly congregated near the players' entrance; phones raised in anticipation. Lauryn and I found a decent vantage point as the sleek black buses pulled up, their tinted windows adding to the mystique of the moment.

The real excitement, however, peaked as two of college football's most prominent players emerged: Shedeur Sanders, Coach Prime's son and the team's dynamic quarterback and Travis Hunter, the nation's former No. 1 overall recruit who played on both offense as a receiver, and on defense as a cornerback. Both stars, now embedded among their teammates, stepped off the buses to thunderous applause. Lauryn, managing to position herself perfectly, captured several clear photos of both phenoms as they made their way into the stadium. The crowd's reaction highlighted the star power these players now brought to Boulder—fans calling out their names, trying to catch their attention, creating the kind of buzz rarely seen at a program that hadn't been in the national spotlight for years.

This was "Coach Prime" effect in full force: what would have been a routine team arrival in previous seasons had transformed into something akin to a red-carpet event. The scene perfectly encapsulated the program's transformation; it brought a touch of Hollywood to the Rockies, merging Colorado's laid-back vibe with Prime Time's ambiance for the dramatic.

After the team disappeared into the stadium, we found ourselves discussing how this simple moment exemplified the changing face of college football: where player personalities and social media presence had become as much a part of the gameday experience as the traditional pageantry.

After the excitement of the team's arrival settled down, we made our way to the Franklin Field Tailgate Zone—a dedicated tailgating area nestled right next to the stadium. Unlike the typical parking lot tailgate scenes I'd experienced elsewhere, this space was laid out with intention. A practice-field-length stretch of artificial turf served as the centerpiece, with designated tailgate stations neatly lining its perimeter. Each setup was remarkably consistent: folding lawn chairs, small BBQ grills, and a steady flow of music and laughter. Each tailgating setup was more of a communal atmosphere that was different from the sprawling parking lot setups I'd seen at other venues.

We wandered through this area, encountering several welcoming groups. Following my now-familiar introduction about the bucket list journey, we found ourselves drawn into various conversations. The mix of fans included Colorado alumni, current students' parents, and quite a few first-time visitors like us who had been drawn in by the Coach Prime phenomenon.

One particular group, a mixture of Colorado and Baylor fans, insisted we join them. As we shared stories, they were particularly interested in hearing about the other venues I'd visited and how Colorado's gameday atmosphere compared. The consensus among the longtime Colorado fans was that while their tailgate scene might be smaller in scale, the recent surge of interest in the program had brought new energy to these pregame gatherings.

Around 4:30 p.m., noting that the tailgate energy had plateaued and feeling the anticipation for kickoff building, we decided to head into the stadium. While the tailgating scene might not have matched the intensity of other venues on my journey, the intimate setting and friendly encounters had provided yet another unique perspective on college football culture.

This stadium with its capacity of just over fifty thousand, offered an intimate setting. Our seats in Section 109, Row 17 (ironically this was the first row), seats 34 and 35 positioned us in the south endzone and to our right-hand side the iconic black endzone ramp with "COLORADO" written in gold. Adjacent to our section was the Colorado Buffaloes band, and we felt their energy and excitement during the entire game.

As game time approached, clouds began to form, and we prepared our rain gear. During pregame warmups, we watched Shedeur Sanders and Travis Hunter from a distance, taking selfies with them in the background. I eagerly anticipated seeing Ralphie, the live bison mascot, bring the team onto the field.

Once inside Folsom Field, Lauryn and I took advantage of our prime location for photos. With the iconic black ramp behind us, and the majestic Rocky Mountains providing a stunning backdrop to the north end zone, we captured several memorable father-daughter shots. The setting sun in an overcast sky cast a perfect light across the stadium, creating picture-perfect moments we knew we'd cherish long after this bucket list journey ended.

From our vantage point, we had an excellent view of pregame warmups, particularly Shedeur Sanders and Travis Hunter. We watched intently as Shedeur went through his throwing progressions, his precision evident even in warmups, while Travis Hunter showed off the athleticism that made him one of college football's most exciting two-way players. Lauryn, always ready with her phone, captured several great shots of both stars as they prepared for the evening's contest.

Just before 6 p.m., the energy in the stadium began to build as the Colorado band took the field, accompanied by cheerleaders. The live bison Raphie's handlers, dressed in distinctively white shirts and black cowboy hats, entered the field as the pre-game ritual took on an added dimension with an air of western authenticity to the opening ceremony.

The video board suddenly came to life with a montage celebrating Ralphie's legacy, building to the iconic "Run, Ralphie, Run!" moment. The crowd was filled with anticipation as we waited for Colorado's unique tradition to unfold. The combination of modern hype videos featuring Coach Prime and his players, mixed with the traditional element of a live mascot, created a fascinating blend of old and new Colorado football culture. It was yet another reminder of how the program was managing to honor its traditions while embracing its high-profile transformation.

The stadium erupted as Ralphie, Colorado's magnificent live bison mascot, thundered onto the field, guided expertly by the handlers. The raw power and speed of the buffalo charging across the field was breathtaking, a tradition that television simply can't do justice. Following this spectacular entrance, the Colorado flag bearers raced onto the field, each carrying a letter to spell out "C-O-L-O-R-A-D-O," their coordinated movements creating a wave of black and gold that led the team through the tunnel as they burst onto the field to deafening cheers.

The game itself proved thrilling, a back-and-forth battle where Baylor took a 24–17 lead into the half. The halftime show featured the marching band forming Deion Sanders's iconic fedora and sunglasses, a creative tribute to their coach. The second half saw increased offensive action; despite Sheduer Sanders being sacked eight times, the Buffaloes hung around long enough to lead a comeback effort as they continued to trail for most of the game.

The fourth quarter brought heavier rain and intense drama. With Baylor leading 31–24, Shedeur Sanders connected with Lajontay Wester for an exciting game-tying touchdown as time expired. In overtime, Colorado scored first, while Travis Hunter sealed the victory for Colorado 38–31 by forcing a fumble that went through the endzone. The premature field-storming and goalpost-lowering only added to the memorable chaos as the officials confirmed the fumble was game ending for the Bears.

As we drove back to Denver in the rain, Lauryn and I reflected on the day. While the tailgating scene might not have matched traditional powerhouse programs, the game's excitement and our time together made it a perfect addition to my bucket list journey. As we parted ways at Denver's airport on Sunday, I was already looking forward to Week Five's adventure to see the Arizona Wildcats take on the Utah Utes in Salt Lake City, a new destination for me to explore.

ARIZONA AT #10 UTAH

Week Five of my journey began with careful planning on August 10th. While considering several attractive matchups—Wisconsin vs. USC, Louisville at Notre Dame, TCU in Kansas, and Big Ten offerings like Illinois vs. Penn State—I ultimately chose Arizona vs. Utah in Salt Lake City. This would be my first time in the state of Utah, and I looked forward to experiencing a different part of the country. I secured my airfare, my hotel (near both the airport and stadium), rental car, and a single game ticket, though the actual game time remained undetermined.

While planning Week Five, I noticed something that would become a recurring theme throughout my bucket list journey—the uncertainty of game times. When I purchased my ticket for the Arizona vs. Utah matchup, the kickoff time wasn't yet established. At first, this struck me as odd; here I was, booking flights, reserving hotels, and arranging rental cars without knowing if I'd be attending a morning, afternoon, or night game.

This uncertainty was likely due to television networks' scheduling strategies. The more attractive or potentially impactful games would often get preferential time slots for maximum viewership; so the time would be announced just a week or so before game day.

I figured I'd be in Salt Lake City regardless of kickoff time, and I'd adjust my plans accordingly once the time was announced. This would become a valuable lesson for future weeks of my bucket list journey: being flexible with game times was just part of the modern college football experience. What mattered more was being there for the full game day experience, from early tailgating to postgame celebrations, regardless of when the actual game began.

As it turned out, we got an 8 p.m. Mountain time kickoff, which worked perfectly with my plans to explore Salt Lake City and experience the full range of pregame activities. This timing would allow me to tour the city in the morning, visit the campus in the afternoon, and still have plenty of time to enjoy the tailgating scene before the evening kickoff.

Arriving in Salt Lake City in the early afternoon on Friday, September 27th, I was immediately struck by the majestic mountain ranges surrounding the city. I couldn't help but imagine how breathtaking they must look capped with snow in winter. After checking into my hotel around 1:30 p.m., I searched for local attractions and decided to explore Big Cottonwood Canyon, about thirty-five miles away. First, I made a quick stop at Walmart to purchase a Utah Utes hat to complement the red shirt I'd brought for game day.

The drive to Big Cottonwood Canyon revealed a landscape surrounded with some residential areas, rental condos for ski season and hiking trails. Around 3:30 p.m., I discovered the Willow Heights Trail, a deceptively challenging 0.75-mile hike with a 600-foot elevation gain. In viewing the map at the beginning of the trail, I noticed what appeared to be a lake toward the end of the hike, which I decided to visit. Dressed casually in a t-shirt, jeans, and Air Jordans, I set out with just a water bottle. The trail rewarded me with stunning views of fall foliage: brilliant greens, oranges, and yellows against the mountain backdrop. The peaceful solitude was broken only by the crunch of rocks beneath my feet. After about forty-five minutes of climbing and several reassurances from passing hikers that I was "getting close," I reached a small, serene body of water around 4:15 p.m. The hike wasn't too tough, but the climb got a little harder with the elevation and the mid-80s heat. The trail didn't have any seating along the entire path, but I rested while finishing up my water before beginning the journey back to my car. The descent proved more challenging than the ascent, as I quickly learned why hikers wear hiking shoes; I felt like I could lose my footing at any moment and fall, as the crushed gravel rocks were slippery. I took it really easy and at times walked down sideways to minimize my chances of slipping and falling. I finally made it back to my car around 5:15 p.m. with the lower part of my jeans and shoes totally covered in dust and dirt.

Once I got back in the car, I realized how hungry I was. And with an impromptu Google search for soul food, I was led to an unexpected gem not too far away in a neighboring town: Sauce Boss Southern Kitchen in Draper, Utah. My first thought was, *There's no way I'm going to get the kind of soul food so prevalent in Southern states here in Utah*. Walking into the crowded restaurant just after 6 p.m., I was greeted with pork rinds and hot sauce as an appetizer: a promising sign and a change from typical table bread, which I've never experienced at any restaurant. The Black-owned establishment delivered an exceptional meal of catfish, mac-n-cheese, collard greens with pepper sauce, and French fries. Though the packed house prevented me from meeting Chef Julius, the food was an undisputed 10 out of 10.

As I returned to the hotel from Sauce Boss, I was treated to a stunning sunset view of the mountains. Once settled in my room, I knew I needed to prepare for what would be a long Saturday, especially with the late 8:15 p.m. kickoff. I took advantage of the hotel's laundry facilities to wash my dust-covered jeans, socks, and shoes from the hiking adventure. While waiting for the laundry, I even had to get creative, using the hair dryer to ensure my shoes would be completely dry for the next day. The rest of Friday evening was spent relaxing in my room, watching college football on TV, and getting some rest. It was the perfect way to wind down, knowing Saturday would be packed with campus exploration, tailgating, and a full night of football ahead.

Saturday morning began at 8 a.m. with hotel breakfast and freshly laundered clothes from the night before. The mid-60s temperature was perfect for exploring downtown's City Creek Center Mall at around 10:30 a.m. The upscale retail complex housed all the major high-end stores you'd expect to find in any major city. What caught my attention was a fall festival taking place at the convention center across the street, with numerous people dressed in costumes adding to the weekend atmosphere. As I walked through the mall, I couldn't help but notice the demographic makeup of Salt Lake City. Being one of the few, if not the only, Black person in the mall at the time, I felt like a "unicorn" in the predominantly white crowd. It wasn't uncomfortable or unwelcoming, just a noticeable difference from what I usually experienced in Texas. Despite the packed parking lot and steady stream of shoppers enjoying the fall festival activities, I was distinctly aware of being in a city with a very different demographic composition than I was used to.

I continued browsing until just after noon, then I headed back to the hotel for an afternoon snack before making my way to campus. While the mall itself was exactly what you'd expect from a modern shopping center, it provided an interesting glimpse into the local population and culture of Salt Lake City.

By 2 p.m., I had arrived at the University of Utah's campus, finding parking about a half mile from the stadium on one of the streets. The campus impressed me with its intimate feel, with an enrollment of just over thirty-five thousand students. Well-maintained grounds, large trees, and manicured lawns created a welcoming atmosphere. An adjacent light rail system provided convenient access for both students and game attendees.

Around 3:30 p.m., I discovered the student union building, a hub of campus activity even on game day. The facility mirrored other universities with its recreational amenities—pool tables, bowling lanes, and video game areas. While the dining facilities and academic sections were closed, the gaming area remained open, complete with TV access. This proved perfect for catching afternoon football, as I settled in to watch games both on the facility's TV and my phone through YouTube TV. I particularly enjoyed watching Mississippi State take on Texas, with Texas ultimately securing the win.

At 5:30 p.m., I ventured out to explore the tailgating scene. My initial impression was underwhelming—a single tent with six chairs in an otherwise empty parking lot. However, after introducing myself to these early tailgaters and sharing my bucket list story, they directed me toward what would become an impressive pregame celebration closer to the stadium.

As I made my way closer to the stadium, about a ten-to-fifteen-minute walk, I came across Tom, a character who embodied the welcoming spirit of Utah football. Dressed in red Utah Utes t-shirt with grey overalls that read "Grill, Eat, Repeat," Tom was working the grill. He wore his black cap on backwards and was surrounded by his regular tailgating crew. Tom was making sliders, but he'd forgotten the buns, much to the amusement of his friends (who wouldn't let him hear the end of it). Despite this minor setback, he immediately offered me one of his sliders. Though I politely declined since I wasn't hungry, his hospitality was genuine.

Tom, looking every bit the seasoned tailgater in his overalls, took time to chat with me and share some local knowledge. He revealed it was homecoming weekend and mentioned the planned "blackout" where fans would wear black instead of the traditional Utah red. While his own tailgate setup was impressive, what made Tom special was his eagerness to enhance my experience. "Hey, we actually are having a really good tailgate over here," he said, "but keep walking towards the stadium and I promise you you're gonna see an entire street filled with a huge tailgate." He described what awaited me: both sides of the street lined with tents, live music, and an atmosphere I wouldn't want to miss.

After taking some photos and videos with Tom and his crew, and checking out some nearby RVs wrapped in Utah Utes logos, I followed his advice. Sure enough, as I continued toward the stadium, I could hear the music growing louder and see the increasing number of tailgate tents Tom had described. His insider tip proved invaluable, leading me to an even more vibrant game day scene than I could have imagined.

Following Tom's guidance, I made my way closer to the stadium. Just as he promised, the scene transformed dramatically. Both sides of the street were lined with an impressive array of tailgate setups, and the music grew louder with each step. The energy and my excitement were picking up. Some tents belonged to local groups while others were sponsored by various vendors, with homecoming alumni signs scattered throughout. By now it was around 5:45 p.m., and the atmosphere was electric.

My attention was drawn to a particularly exclusive-looking setup: the ESPN 700 AM radio tent. Unlike other tailgates, this one was walled off from general foot traffic, with staff wearing badges controlling access at the entrance. Taking a chance, I approached and introduced myself to a man and woman at the entrance, sharing my story about being a first-time visitor from Texas on Week Five of my fourteen-week bucket list journey. To my surprise, the woman immediately said, "Let me have your wrist," reaching for a wristband. "You've got to come inside," she insisted with heightened enthusiasm.

Once inside, I was escorted to my first stop: James, a gentleman wearing a Clear Water Distilling Company shirt who turned out to be one of the company's founders. He shared the fascinating history of their business, explaining how they were among the first distilleries permitted in Utah County. James offered me a sample of their signature spirit: a smooth, cinnamon-infused drink that was absolutely delicious.

The hospitality continued as I was introduced to Scott, one of the co-founders of Wingers, a local wing establishment. Their setup was impressive, offering chicken tenders, loaded mashed potatoes, and quesadillas. The sauces were exceptional, particularly their homemade ranch, which lived up to their claim of having "the best wings and the best sauces." Scott was gracious enough to take some selfies with me and share stories about their business.

The ESPN tent proved to be an unexpected highlight of my tailgating experience, offering not just great food and drinks, but a chance to meet local business owners and experience true Utah hospitality. What started as a simple introduction at the entrance had turned into an exclusive game day experience. I never anticipated.

One of my next memorable encounters was with Marcus from Miss Essie's Southern BBQ. His setup and crew were immediately welcoming, inviting me to sample their food and drinks. I spent about fifteen to twenty minutes hanging out with Marcus and his group, during which he made sure to dispel any misconceptions I might have had about Utah being a dry state. "Salt Lake City is certainly not a dry city," he assured me with a laugh, encouraging me to enjoy some of his libations—an offer I gladly accepted.

As I continued exploring, the tailgating scene kept growing more impressive. I came across a Utah Utes party bus with a band playing on top: a spectacle I hadn't expected. Adjacent to this was a courtyard with its own live music, creating multiple pockets of entertainment and energy throughout the area.

In the midst of all the Utah red and black, I ran into two guys from Houston who stood out in their Arizona gear. They were there supporting family members playing for Arizona, and we immediately connected over our Texas roots. What started as a quick hello turned into a good five- or ten-minute conversation, as they too were fascinated by my bucket list journey story. It was one of those organic moments that make college football special: finding common ground with fellow fans, even those supporting the opposing team, and sharing stories about what brought us all to this place on this particular Saturday.

These diverse encounters—from Marcus's local barbecue hospitality to the traveling Arizona fans from my home state—highlighted how college football brings people together, creating unexpected connections and memorable moments far from home.

By around 7 p.m., the tailgate celebration reached a new level of excitement with the arrival of the Utah marching band. They made their entrance in parade fashion, weaving through the tailgate area with high-energy performances that immediately amplified the game day atmosphere. The sight of their red and black uniforms, coupled with the sound of their instruments echoing off the surrounding buildings and mountains, created a magical college football moment.

All around the tailgate area, fans stopped what they were doing, gravitating toward the music. The band's presence seemed to signal that game time was approaching, and you could feel the excitement building among the crowd. Adding to the spectacle were the numerous twenty-foot flag poles scattered throughout the area, the Utes team logo waving prominently against the evening sky.

The band's march through the tailgate section served as a perfect transition from the pregame festivities to the main event, effectively rallying fans to start making their way toward Rice-Eccles Stadium. It was another example of the rich game day traditions that make college football special, and Utah's execution of this tradition was particularly impressive.

Around 7:20, after a fantastic tailgating experience, I began my walk toward Rice-Eccles Stadium. The timing was perfect as the setting sun cast a beautiful glow against the mountain backdrop, creating a picturesque scene. Though the stadium, which holds just over fifty-one thousand fans, was only about a fifteen-minute walk away, each step revealed new views that made the journey memorable.

As I entered the stadium, I came upon something unexpected and impressive: the Olympic cauldron. This massive structure stood as a proud reminder of Salt Lake City's role as host of the 2002 Winter Olympics and Winter Paralympics Games. Standing there, looking at this piece of Olympic history, I couldn't help but reflect on the broader significance of where I was. The cauldron served as a powerful symbol of both athletic achievement and the city's heritage, adding another layer of meaning to my visit.

The whole approach to the stadium, mountains in the background, the setting sun, and this Olympic monument, made me appreciate how college football venues often connect to their communities in deeper ways. It wasn't just about the game; it was about the history, the landscape, and the people who made this place special. I found myself pausing to reflect on how the tailgate experience I'd just enjoyed exemplified this: strangers coming together, sharing food, drinks, and stories, all without concern for political affiliations or ideologies. It was pure celebration and community, exactly what college football should be. My inner voice reflected on all this: *I wasn't expecting to unpack these types of thoughts and experiences by coming to games, it's a pure by-product.*

Around 7:30 p.m., I settled into my seat in section S3, row 32, seat 10. The setting was spectacular, with the mountains creating a stunning backdrop against the single-tier stadium. Despite being a "blackout" game where fans were encouraged to wear black, my red attire didn't make me feel out of place.

One of the most distinctive features of Rice-Eccles Stadium was the impressive display of twenty-foot Utah Utes flags that fans flew on telescopic poles. Unlike anything I'd seen at other venues, these massive flagpoles were engineered to be lowered between plays, allowing fans to maintain their view while keeping the flags as part of the game day atmosphere. These flags, bearing Utah's colors and symbols, added a unique element to the stadium's character and became an integral part of the University of Utah's game day persona.

The pregame festivities brought traditional college football energy, with the cheerleaders and band marching onto the field while the JumboTron displayed a varied array of promotional content and hype videos to energize the crowd. The coordination between the band's music, the cheerleaders' routines, and the crowd's enthusiasm created that classic college football atmosphere I'd come to love on this journey.

I struck up a conversation with Wade, a friendly local fan seated to my right with his family. Like many others I'd met that day, he was intrigued by my bucket list quest and shared his own insights about Utah football traditions. As the game progressed, Wade explained one of Utah's most moving traditions: the fourth-quarter tribute to two former players lost to gun violence. As the third quarter came to a close, an announcement came over the PA system, and the stadium lights dimmed. On cue, nearly fifty-thousand fans raised their cell phones, activating their flashlights to illuminate the night sky. The sea of lights created a stunning visual memorial, transforming the stadium into a constellation of bright points against the dark mountain backdrop. It was a powerful moment of unity and remembrance that transcended the game itself, demonstrating how football can bring people together in meaningful ways.

The game itself wasn't the competitive matchup many expected, with Arizona largely controlling both sides of the ball. Utah, ranked #10 at the time, was playing at a disadvantage with their starting quarterback sidelined by injury. Their freshman quarterback, despite his efforts, struggled to find rhythm against Arizona's defense. The combination of offensive mistakes and Arizona's strong defensive showing led to a 23–10 victory for the unranked Wildcats.

As the game wound down and Utah's chances of a comeback dwindled, fans began filing out with about five minutes left on the clock.

I decided to stay put, partly to avoid the exit rush but also because I wanted to get one of the Utah Utes souvenir cups I'd had my eye on that fans would surely leave behind. It proved to be a smart decision. While others rushed to their cars, I took my time, secured my souvenir, and had a leisurely twenty-minute walk back to my parking spot.

One of the impressive aspects of Utah's game day operations became clear during the exit: the light rail system proved invaluable. I could see streams of fans heading toward the trains, which significantly reduced the vehicle traffic leaving the stadium area. Thanks to this efficient system and my delayed departure, my drive back to the hotel was surprisingly smooth, taking no more than thirty minutes.

This defeat for Utah may not have been the outcome the home crowd wanted, but it didn't diminish what had been an incredible game day experience. The weather had been perfect, the tailgating scene had far exceeded my expectations, and I'd gotten much more out of this trip than I'd anticipated. As I drove back to the hotel, I reflected on how Salt Lake City had thoroughly impressed me with its scenery, hospitality, and college football atmosphere. Week Five was coming to a close, and my thoughts were already turning to Week Six. I was excited to return to familiar territory with a Friday night game in Texas where The University of Houston Cougars would take on the TCU Horned Frogs in Fort-Worth.

HOUSTON AT TCU

Week Six of my journey began with random thoughts during my August 10th planning session. While enticing matchups like Auburn at Georgia and UCLA at Penn State caught my attention, I ultimately settled on a Friday night showdown between the University of Houston and TCU in Fort Worth. The Georgia game was particularly tempting, but I had hopes of catching the Bulldogs later in the season. What made the TCU game especially appealing was its timing: a Friday night contest on October 4th that aligned perfectly with my technology sales work in Dallas. I could visit a customer in Dallas during the morning, then head to Fort Worth for the afternoon and evening festivities.

The decision was further sweetened by a personal connection: my friend Glynn's son Braylon was a redshirt freshman on TCU's team. ("Redshirt" is a term used to describe college athletes who forgo their participation in games during their first year to extend their eligibility.) This would give me an opportunity to support them both—Braylon as a young player navigating his college journey and Glynn as a proud father—while experiencing some Friday night football in

Texas. College football creates an opportunity to celebrate the journey of student-athletes and being there is an opportunity to cheer the team on even if it wasn't in the form of touchdowns or game time. The Friday scheduling also meant I could return home for the majority of the weekend instead of traveling back on Sunday like my other trips. After settling on my choice, I reached out to Glynn, who graciously offered to handle my game ticket arrangements.

On the morning of October 4th, after wrapping up my business meeting in Dallas, I made my way to Fort Worth, arriving at TCU's campus just after 12:30 p.m. Knowing it was still an active school day, I strategically avoided the campus parking areas. Instead, I scouted the adjacent neighborhoods, hoping I could find street parking before any potential game day parking restrictions went into effect. My strategy paid off; I found a spot in a residential area about a twenty-minute walk from campus, saving both money and the hassle of navigating campus parking.

From my first steps onto TCU's grounds, I was struck by the distinct character of this private institution. The three-hundred-acre campus exuded an upscale, meticulously maintained atmosphere that seamlessly blended contemporary energy with established tradition. Impeccably manicured lawns spread between administrative buildings and dormitories, while mature trees provided shade along immaculate sidewalks. What caught my attention immediately was the student body's surprising diversity, a notable observation for a prestigious private school historically known for its predominantly Caucasian enrollment and substantial tuition costs.

The campus was alive with typical Friday activity. Fraternity and sorority members gathered in groups, students traversed the paths on various modes of transportation from skateboards to e-scooters, and others took advantage of the beautiful fall weather by studying or socializing on the lawn areas. This vibrant scene of campus life played out against a backdrop of impressive architecture and thoughtfully designed spaces, making it clear why TCU had earned its reputation as one of Texas's premier private universities.

While exploring campus in my purple polo shirt, I made my way to the campus bookstore, which I discovered was strategically located in a bustling student center. The center served as a natural gathering spot, housing not only the bookstore but also familiar favorites like Starbucks and Chick-fil-A, alongside the adjacent main student cafeteria. The timing of my visit—early afternoon—meant the area was buzzing with students grabbing lunch and generic college student talk.

Inside the bookstore, I searched for something to complement my purple polo, ultimately settling on a TCU hat that perfectly matched my shirt's color. The store was well-stocked with game day gear, and there was already a noticeable excitement building for the evening's contest, even among the staff and students shopping for regular supplies.

After securing my TCU gear, I decided to grab lunch at the Chick-fil-A. The student center's dining area provided an excellent vantage point for people-watching and absorbing the campus atmosphere. Students filled the tables, many discussing their plans for the evening's game, while others hurried to afternoon classes. The energy was different from what you might find on a typical game day, as this was still very much an active school day transitioning into a football Friday.

The combination of the bustling student center, well-appointed bookstore, and variety of dining options reflected TCU's commitment to creating comfortable, modern spaces for their student body.

It was clear this wasn't just a place for quick transactions, but a true community hub where student life and school spirit intersected.

As I continued my campus exploration, the beauty of early fall in Fort Worth revealed itself with each step. The changing season painted the campus in a spectacular array of colors, with an especially fitting touch: hints of TCU purple naturally woven into the fall foliage. These purple hues, mixed with traditional autumn oranges and yellows, created a stunning contrast against the backdrop of the campus's established but refreshed buildings. The mature trees that lined the walkways were just beginning their seasonal transformation, creating perfect photo opportunities for me throughout the grounds.

During my wanderings, I came upon one of TCU's most iconic landmarks: the horned frog statue. This wasn't just any mascot statue; it was a beautifully crafted piece that captured the unique character of TCU's unusual but beloved mascot. The horned frog is actually a spiky blood-squirting lizard and has become a symbol of the university's resilience and distinct character. The sculpture sat prominently positioned, making it a natural photo spot for visitors and students alike. I took advantage of the opportunity to capture several photos, including some selfies with the horned frog. The statue's placement was perfect, with the fall colors and historic campus buildings creating an ideal backdrop that encapsulated everything distinct about TCU.

The whole scene—the horned frog statue, the purple-tinged fall foliage, and the academic-modern buildings—created a perfect representation of TCU's blend of tradition and natural beauty. It was one of those moments that reminded me why in-person visits to these campuses were so special; no television broadcast or website could capture the genuine character of a campus on a beautiful fall afternoon.

Around 4 p.m., I discovered what would become one of the day's highlights: TCU's Frog Alley coming to life. Located in the heart of campus, this pregame festival area was being transformed into what felt like a community celebration rather than just a typical tailgate. Crews were setting up stages for live music and inflating bounce houses for children. Food trucks were rolling into their designated spots. An atmosphere was being created that promised something for everyone.

Frog Alley struck me as TCU's answer to an inclusive game day experience. Unlike traditional tailgating, which might be scattered across parking lots or limited to private groups, this was clearly designed as a gathering space where everyone—students, alumni, families, and visiting fans—could come together. The setup was impressive: vendors arranging their booths, sound systems being tested, and event staff preparing for the crowds that would soon arrive.

The excitement reached a new level around 4:30 p.m. when the team buses pulled up. This carefully choreographed arrival tradition drew crowds of fans who lined up to watch the players make their walk from Frog Alley to the stadium. It was a perfect example of how college football traditions can bring a community together: students paused their activities, families positioned their children for better views, and alumni stood proudly as the team made their entrance.

The whole scene had a festival-like quality that felt distinctly TCU. Rather than the typical parking lot tailgate experience, Frog Alley offered a more curated, family-friendly atmosphere while still maintaining the excitement of college football game day. The beautiful fall weather only enhanced the experience, with the late afternoon sun casting a perfect light over the growing crowd of purple-clad fans.

While exploring Frog Alley, I came across Ken, one of those memorable characters that make college football special. His tailgate setup caught my attention, but it was his welcoming personality that made the encounter memorable. Ken had an impressive spread, featuring grilled steaks, and wasn't shy about sharing his cinnamon-infused Fireball whiskey. In a perfect moment of synchronicity, Pitbull's "Fireball" was playing from his speakers as he offered me a Fireball shot. Ken's hospitality embodied the spirit of college football tailgating: strangers becoming instant friends over food, drinks, and shared excitement for the game. As had become my custom, I captured a video with Ken while sharing my bucket list journey story, which he found fascinating.

After spending time at Ken's tailgate, I noticed an area designated specifically for players' families. Following my instinct to introduce myself, I approached the group and met Mr. Carroll, father of two sons who were redshirt freshman on the TCU team. When I mentioned my connection to Glynn, whose son was also on the team, Mr. Carroll immediately made me feel welcome. The players' family tailgate had a different energy from the other setups: there was an underlying sense of personal investment in the evening's game, with parents sharing stories about their sons and their journeys to TCU football.

Moving between these two distinct tailgate experiences—Ken's enthusiastic hospitality and the more intimate family atmosphere of the players' tailgate—offered different but equally authentic perspectives on TCU football culture. The area around us continued to buzz with activity, as music played from various tailgate setups, and young kids tossed footballs around, all while families enjoyed the perfect fall evening weather. These interactions exemplified how college football brings together different groups of people, from passionate fans like Ken to proud parents like Mr. Carroll, all united by their connection to TCU.

Around 5:30 p.m., I finally connected with Glynn, who was easy to spot in his full TCU game day attire. He was in his element, engaged in conversation with other football parents, sharing stories and pre-game excitement. After catching up and taking some photos together, our timing proved perfect as the TCU band began their entrance into Frog Alley around 5:40 p.m. The drummers led the way, their cadence drawing fans toward the procession and building excitement as everyone began gravitating toward the stadium.

By 5:45 p.m., Glynn and I decided it was time to make our way to Amon Carter Stadium. The venue itself was impressive: a forty-six thousand-capacity facility featuring a unique design with three tiers of seating along the sidelines and two tiers in the end zones. For a school with just under eleven thousand students, the stadium created an intimate yet striking atmosphere that felt perfectly scaled for TCU football.

Glynn had secured us excellent seats in section 128, part of the players' family general admission area. Our location, situated on the sideline adjacent to the end zone, offered a fantastic vantage point for the evening's action.

As we settled into our spots, I took the time to absorb the stadium's atmosphere. iPhone video and stills captured the stadium lighting peeking above the setting sun, the tiered mix of bleacher and purple padded seating that wrapped around the field, as well as their endzone JumboTron seated on arches. The interior walls displayed the program's achievements, with conference and national championship years proudly displayed for all to see.

The setting sun cast a beautiful light across the field, and the energy was building despite the stands being less than half full, not surprising for a Friday evening when many fans were still making their way from work or school.

The stadium's intimate design meant that even with the gradually filling stands, you felt close to the action from anywhere in the venue. This was exactly the kind of setting that made college football special: a perfect blend of modern amenities while maintaining a connection to the tradition and scale of college football.

Around 6:30 p.m., the pregame festivities kicked into high gear as the TCU band lined up in one of the far end zones. The cheerleaders joined them, creating the traditional tunnel formation while energizing the still-filling stadium. The atmosphere built to a crescendo as the football team emerged through a cloud of smoke, with the band's music reaching a powerful climax.

The game's first half belonged entirely to the University of Houston, who dominated TCU en route to a 24–6 halftime lead. During the break, I experienced an unexpected reunion. Earlier, I had reached out to my former coworker Eric, letting him know I was at the game where his son Coleton was now a student. Despite not having seen him in seven or eight years, we arranged to meet in the concourse. After catching up and sending a photo to Eric, his son shared an interesting insight into student culture at TCU: he and his friends were leaving at halftime, an apparently common practice among students who often treated games more as social events than sporting contests.

The second half maintained the same trajectory as the first, with TCU fighting hard but unable to overcome their turnovers and Houston's consistent performance. However, the third quarter brought one of the evening's most memorable moments: an innovative drone show that illuminated the night sky directly above the end zone. The drones choreographed themselves to spell out "Fear the Frog," and "Go Frogs" in brilliant purple lights, creating a spectacular visual display I'd never experienced at a football game before.

Adding to the unique atmosphere was TCU's touchdown celebration tradition: a vehicle in the end zone equipped with a train horn that would blast after each Horned Frogs score. The horn's thunderous sound echoed throughout the stadium, though we didn't hear it as often as the home crowd would have liked that night.

As the fourth quarter wound down, Houston secured their victory with a final score of 30–19. Despite TCU's loss, the evening had delivered everything that makes college football special: tradition, innovation in the form of the drone show, and the opportunity to share the experience with both old friends like Glynn and new acquaintances in the family section. As I prepared for the three-hour drive home, my mind was already drifting to Week Seven's upcoming adventure in Eugene, Oregon, but not before appreciating how TCU had provided a perfect example of Friday Night Texas football hospitality, even on a challenging night for the home team.

#2 OHIO STATE AT #3 OREGON

As July turned to August 2024, I began evaluating potential Week Seven destinations. Albuquerque caught my eye with Air Force taking on New Mexico, offering a chance to experience the unique Southwestern culture. Other attractive options included Florida at Tennessee for classic SEC action, and Mississippi State at Georgia (though I was considering saving Georgia for a later visit). The Ohio State at Oregon matchup was enticing, but Eugene's limited lodging options and steep airfare prices initially made it seem impractical. The UCLA-Minnesota game at the Rose Bowl also tempted me, but fate had other plans.

During an August 19th video call with a customer of mine named Jason, fate stepped in through an amusing coincidence: I happened to be wearing my bright green polo shirt while Jason appeared on screen sporting an Oregon Ducks polo. This simple matching of our shirts completely transformed our typically formal business discussion. For the first time, we spent the entire call on a personal level, where I learned about his deep connection to Oregon. Jason shared that he was a University of Oregon alum who hadn't missed a home game in years, frequently traveled to away games, and maintained a long-standing tailgate tradition with family and friends. His excitement about the upcoming season was contagious. When I mentioned my bucket list and how I'd considered the Ohio State game but found the costs prohibitive, his eyes lit up. Without hesitation, he extended an invitation to join his tailgate, mentioning that several executives from his company and business partners would be there—a perfect opportunity for networking. My excitement soared, my internal Whitlock said, *Hell yeah, this is the Week Seven game I'm going to.* Jason gave me the insider's tip to assist with cheaper lodging and airfare, which meant flying into Portland and driving to Eugene (about 120 miles) rather than trying to fly directly into Eugene. His promise to take good care of me sealed the deal.

On August 22nd, I finalized my arrangements, booking flights to Portland (following Jason's insider tip about avoiding Eugene's airport), securing downtown lodging, reserving a rental car and solidifying my game ticket. I also purchased an Oregon Ducks hat online to complement my lucky green polo. I flew out early on Friday October 11th, arriving in Portland late morning. I kept my first day low-key, staying mostly in the downtown area to rest up for Saturday's adventures in Eugene.

My game day began at 5:45 a.m. with what had become my traditional ritual: recording a video message to share with family and friends back home. As I headed down to the lobby, I found myself sharing the elevator with several Ohio State fans decked out in their scarlet and gray gear. Their energy was infectious, and when they asked about my green polo, I shared my bucket list journey with them. Their reaction was authentic and heartwarming; this was not just polite interest but real excitement about my mission to experience college football's greatest venues and matchups. One fan was so moved by my story that he insisted I join their alumni breakfast at the neighboring hotel, an invitation I respectfully declined in order to stay on schedule. The brief elevator encounter perfectly captured what I'd come to love about college football: how complete strangers could form an instant connection over their shared passion for the game, regardless of team allegiances. As I entered the lobby, I was struck by the sea of scarlet. Ohio State fans had shown up in force, living up to their reputation as one of college football's most dedicated traveling fan bases.

Jason told me his tailgate spot was at the Masonic Lodge, really close to the stadium; so I programmed that into my GPS and embarked on the two-hour drive to Eugene. I reached Eugene around 8:30 a.m., fully aware that ESPN College GameDay was in town for this clash between #2 Ohio State and #3 Oregon—both undefeated powerhouses. Despite this being my fourth GameDay experience of the season, I was more focused on the practical matter of finding parking near the Masonic Lodge where Jason's tailgate would be. After passing the lodge itself, I continued down to Kinsrow Avenue, eventually finding a perfect street parking spot in an area dominated by student apartments. Rather than walking into campus, I decided to take a ten-minute Uber ride to maximize my morning exploration time. My driver, Billy, proved to be a friendly local who knew exactly where to drop me for the best campus access. By 9:20 a.m., I found myself stepping out onto E. 13th Avenue, a typical college town street lined with bars, bookstores, and coffee shops. Billy had picked the perfect spot, positioning me right across from the main campus entrance, setting me up perfectly for my morning adventure at the University of Oregon. Jason let me know he and his tailgate crew would likely attend GameDay but I could come by the tailgate spot anytime. I let him know that I'd check out campus for a bit and then come find them a little later in the morning.

As I stepped onto the three-hundred-acre campus, home to roughly twenty-five thousand students, I found myself amid a steady stream of students and fans returning from the GameDay broadcast. The morning air was crisp, hovering in the low 60s, with a mix of Oregon green and Ohio State scarlet dotting the crowd. The campus's first impression was stunning: a blend of historic and modern architecture, dominated by red brick, merged seamlessly with its abundant botanical landscape. I paused at the entrance to capture my first selfie of the day, positioning myself in front of a university sign elegantly embedded within a red brick column. While GameDay had wrapped up its broadcast, the set was still intact, and that's when I witnessed one of those uniquely college football moments: an older gentleman with flowing gray hair and matching beard standing beside a llama of similar height and coloring. This peculiar pair, who I later learned were Larry and his therapy llama, Cesar, made for an unexpected but perfectly fitting addition to the Oregon game day atmosphere. The whole scene captured the essence of college football: architectural footprints with timeless designs quietly providing told stories of the universities past, excited fans, and those wonderfully weird traditions that make each campus unique.

At 9:30 a.m., my campus exploration revealed an unexpected passion I never knew I had. As I came across the bronze Oregon duck statue, I found myself increasingly captivated not by the mascot, but by the stunning arboreal display surrounding me. The campus was a living museum of over four thousand trees, each seemingly positioned with perfect precision. What struck me most was the extraordinary palette of autumn colors—brilliant reds and vibrant yellows reaching toward the sky, creating a natural canopy that seemed almost orchestrated in its beauty. I'd never considered myself particularly interested in trees before, but the sheer magnitude of their height, presence and the breathtaking display of fall colors sparked something new in me. Curiosity led me to pull out my phone, using Google Lens to identify these magnificent specimens. I found myself sitting beneath a particularly stunning purple leaf European beech tree, diving deep into the university's dedicated webpage about their campus trees. While continuing on my walk, I came upon the Knight Library, and it hit me: I was in Nike country. The library's name served as a reminder that this was Phil Knight's territory, the Nike founder whose influence permeated the campus. The convergence of natural beauty and corporate legacy created a unique atmosphere that felt distinctly Oregon.

The morning unfolded with more campus exploration. By 10 a.m., I returned to the GameDay setup in the business complex courtyard, capturing selfies with the main stage backdrop and a field goal post used for Pat McAfee's field goal challenge. This backdrop was complete with an ironically placed red and golden yellow buckeye tree— a living testament to a wager among governors. Before the 1958 Rose Bowl, the governors of Ohio and Oregon made a friendly bet: the losing state would send a native tree to the winner's university. Though Ohio State won the game, Ohio's governor, who was impressed with Oregon's performance, sent this buckeye tree to Eugene. Now that's what I call mutual respect and goodwill!

After exploring the campus, I found a peaceful spot in the student union's outdoor seating area, surrounded by towering red maples and other majestic trees. But it was my next stop that truly stirred my emotions: Hayward Field. As a longtime track and field enthusiast, I knew I was standing on hallowed ground. This wasn't just any stadium; this was America's temple of track and field, a venue that had hosted countless national championships, Olympic trials, and legendary performances that shaped the sport's history. The new facility, with its striking silver architecture, took my breath away. The design masterfully incorporated a tower resembling an Olympic torch, a fitting tribute to the venue's prestigious past. While I couldn't go inside, even viewing the exterior filled me with awe; this was where legends had been made, and records had been shattered: like Sydney Mclaughlin-Levrone's 400m hurdle world record in the 2024 U.S. track and field Olympic Trials.

The stadium's surroundings matched its grandeur, with meticulously maintained grounds that spoke to Oregon's commitment to athletic excellence. Adjacent to Hayward Field, I discovered a sprawling complex of intramural fields, a testament to the university's dedication to all levels of athletics. These facilities offered everything from soccer and field hockey to tennis courts, and as I watched students engaged in a casual game of frisbee golf, I could sense how seamlessly athletics was woven into daily campus life. The entire scene— from the world-class stadium to the recreational fields—painted a picture of a university where sporting heritage and student life coexisted in perfect harmony.

Around 11 a.m., I noticed a group of about twenty people who appeared to be on a campus tour. Without hesitation, I blended into the group, following them into what turned out to be the Student Recreation Center—and what a revelation that was! From the moment I stepped inside, it was clear this wasn't your typical college gym; this was a Nike-backed testament to athletic excellence. The entrance itself set the tone with its stunning day-lit architecture, providing natural lighting, and welcoming atmosphere. Before even reaching the workout areas, I was impressed by the thoughtfully designed social spaces, complete with comfortable seating areas and large TV screens throughout the facility.

But the real magic lay in the athletic amenities. The rock climbing walls seemed to stretch endlessly upward, while workout studios for every imaginable fitness activity were strategically located within the space. The weight-lifting areas extended as far as the eye could see, with state-of-the-art equipment that would make professional training facilities envious. The aquatic center featured both a recreational pool and a separate lap pool for serious swimmers. Every detail, from the equipment selection to the facility layout, screamed world-class. I couldn't help but think, *Of course it's this impressive—when Nike puts its resources behind something, they don't hold back.* This wasn't just a campus gym; it was a comprehensive wellness complex that could rival any premium fitness facility in the world. The facility perfectly embodied Oregon's commitment to athletic excellence at every level, from casual fitness enthusiasts to elite athletes.

As I prepared to leave the recreation center and head to Jason's tailgate, I had my "aha" moment: Autzen Stadium wasn't on campus at all. This realization instantly transported me back to my South Carolina experience, where I'd encountered a similar setup and wondered about how this affected the student game day experience. While my Uber ride earlier had taken about ten minutes, I suspected there must be a more direct route for students and fans on foot. A quick online search revealed a hidden gem—a scenic pathway connecting campus to the stadium via the riverfront parkway and fields.

What I discovered was far more than just a walkway. This mile-long journey was a natural wonderland that began with an enormous inflatable Oregon duck, perfect for photo opportunities. The Nissan Heisman House setup added to the game day atmosphere, but it was the natural elements that made this walk truly special. The path led me across a bridge spanning the Willamette River, where the sound of flowing water created a peaceful backdrop. I found myself thinking about the thousands of students and fans who must take this walk on game days, how this serene journey could calm pregame jitters or provide a moment of reflection after victories and defeats alike.

The tree-lined pathway offered constant reminders of Oregon's natural beauty, and as I neared the end of the trail, Autzen Stadium revealed itself in dramatic fashion. The iconic yellow "O" Oregon Ducks' logo with its black backdrop commanded attention, while the stadium's gently curved roofline seated above the concrete façade blended harmoniously with the surrounding landscape. It wasn't just a stadium entrance; it was the culmination of a journey that perfectly married natural beauty with athletic tradition. I paused to take it all in, appreciating how this thoughtful design transformed what could have been a simple walk into an integral part of the game day experience.

My arrival at the Masonic Lodge parking lot stopped me in my tracks. *Wow* was all I could initially muster. The expansive lot was a celebration of Oregon football culture, featuring an impressive array of vehicles from full-size bus RVs to pickup trucks and smaller recreational vehicles. Every available space was transformed into a tailgating haven, with tents, TV setups, and cornhole boards scattered throughout. The sound of music and laughter mixed with the scent of various grills, while fans in green and yellow (with patches of Ohio State scarlet mixed in) created a festive atmosphere. The surrounding trees, reminiscent of those on campus, added a natural canopy to this unique venue.

Jason's setup was impossible to miss: his bus RV was a shrine to Oregon football. The entire front windshield served as a display case, showcasing an impressive collection of Oregon football helmets arranged with precision. Oregon and American flags proudly adorned the exterior, marking his territory. His prime spot was flanked by equally impressive setups: a similar-sized bus on one side and a large fifth-wheel RV on the other. All three spaces were unified by Oregon green and yellow tents, creating a welcoming communal area complete with TVs broadcasting early games and comfortable lawn chairs scattered throughout.

The moment I spotted Jason, our business relationship transformed into something entirely different. His booming "SCO DUCKS!" greeting and subsequent bro hug felt like reuniting with an old friend rather than meeting a business associate. The formal barriers of our previous interactions melted away as he immediately began introducing me to his wife and an extensive circle of friends and family. As he shared my bucket list story with the group, I could feel the genuine warmth and interest from everyone present. The professional distance that had characterized our earlier interactions was completely gone, replaced by the kind of camaraderie that college football so often creates.

Among the many introductions, meeting Krista stood out as particularly special. She stood there in her black Oregon jersey with yellow trim, a striking sight alongside her two sons who proudly wore their Ohio State jerseys—a visual representation of divided loyalties united by love of college football. Her story fascinated me: she had met Jason during Oregon's 2021 visit to Columbus, where she caught his attention as a rare Oregon fan in Buckeye territory. That chance encounter led to them exchanging information with Jason extending an open invitation to his tailgate should she ever make it to Eugene.

Now here she was, experiencing Eugene for the first time, just as I was. While she hadn't formally labeled this as a bucket list trip, I couldn't help but notice the parallels to my own journey: traveling across the country to experience a different college football culture, immersing herself in new traditions, and creating lasting memories with her family. As we shared our first-time-in-Oregon experiences, our conversation naturally drifted to future games. When I mentioned my planned trip to Columbus later in the season for the Ohio State–Nebraska game, her eyes lit up. Without hesitation, she offered to host me at her family's tailgate, even pulling out her phone to exchange contact information. This impromptu connection perfectly embodied what I loved about my bucket list journey—how complete strangers could become instant friends through shared passion for college football, leading to future adventures and experiences.

My conversation with Ryan and his wife, Inga, unfolded naturally when he overheard me mentioning Houston. He jumped in, sharing his own connections to the Texas area, and we instantly bonded over our shared Texas experiences, trading familiar references to locations and memories we both knew well. But it was my bucket list story that truly captured Ryan's attention. His eyes widened with enthusiasm as I shared the details of my journey, and I could see his mind working as he listened.

Mid-conversation, Ryan's excitement bubbled over. "You know," he said, leaning in with the air of someone about to share a special secret, "I have a couple tailgate spots at the stadium that I'd love to take you to. There are some folks there who would absolutely love to hear your story." The sincerity in his voice and his desire to enrich my Oregon experience was impossible to resist. His wife Inga shared his enthusiasm, and as they discussed their own family—including their kids' sports experiences and their daughter who attended the University of Oregon—I knew this impromptu tour would be something special.

As I agreed to join them, Ryan's face lit up with the satisfaction of someone who knew he was about to add an unexpected chapter to someone else's adventure. His excitement wasn't just about showing off more tailgates; it was about connecting a fellow football enthusiast with a broader community of fans who shared the same passion. This spontaneous invitation would prove to be one of the day's most memorable turns, leading to experiences I couldn't have planned or anticipated.

The walk to the stadium parking lot with Ryan led to an extraordinary series of encounters, beginning with Ms. Carol's elaborate tailgate setup. As Ryan made the introduction, Ms. Carol's welcoming personality immediately shone through. Before I could finish sharing my bucket list story, she was already ushering me under their massive tent, decorated meticulously in Oregon's green and yellow. Everything from the plates to cups to chairs coordinated perfectly in team colors, showcasing her attention to detail.

The spread was unlike any tailgate food I'd encountered: gourmet seafood tacos with all the fixings, a delicious departure from traditional tailgate fare. But what truly set Ms. Carol's tailgate apart was the innovative "Down Shot" tradition. She proudly showed off their custom-modified football down marker, cleverly engineered with four cutouts for shot glasses— their unique take on the traditional "ShotSki" concept used in ski lodges. With infectious enthusiasm, Ms.

Carol insisted I participate. Soon enough, I found myself alongside her, her daughter, and Ryan, taking our "first down" shot in perfect unison. The second "down" followed shortly after, accompanied by more amazing food and laughter.

The gathering at Ms. Carol's grew as more people joined, each fascinated by my bucket list journey. Their questions were thoughtful and varied: some wanted to know the logistics, others were curious about how I convinced my wife to support such an ambitious undertaking, and many wanted comparisons between Oregon and other venues. One gentleman carefully approached a more personal question, delicately asking if there was a specific reason for embarking on this journey now. I appreciated his tactful approach and assured him that while it was indeed a bucket list, it wasn't health-motivated.

The surprises continued as Ryan introduced me to someone he simply called "coach." I assumed this was a former youth sports coach of his children, and we posed for a quick selfie. As we walked to the next tailgate, Ryan casually mentioned that I'd just met Oregon's head baseball coach and Nike's head of college football—a revelation that left me momentarily speechless.

Our final stop was what Ryan called "the neighborhood" tailgate, populated by his actual neighbors. The setup rivaled Ms. Carol's, complete with tacos, pizza, and music creating an inviting atmosphere. Here, I met Trevor, whose enthusiasm for my bucket list journey was unmatched. He treated me like a visiting celebrity, declaring my college football quest "the coolest thing he'd ever heard of." His adrenaline-filled excitement and endless questions added yet another memorable character to this remarkable day.

Around 2:30, Ryan and I made our way back to Ms. Carol's tailgate for our ceremonial "third down" shot. The timing couldn't have been more perfect; as we approached, members of the University of Oregon band had gathered at her tent. The musicians, in full uniform, broke into a spirited rendition of "Happy Birthday" in honor of Ms. Carol's upcoming special day. The celebration reached its peak when they transitioned straight into the Oregon fight song, "Mighty Oregon," creating one of those magical game day moments that can't be scripted.

After completing our "third down," we gathered for the final "fourth down" shot around 3 p.m. Just as we finished, the distinct sound of *vroom, vroom* caught my attention. Ryan's eyes lit up with excitement. "Come on," he said, "I want to introduce you to someone special." We walked over to find a striking green and black Harley Davidson motorcycle—but this wasn't just any bike. This was *the* motorcycle responsible for one of Oregon's most iconic game day traditions: leading the Duck mascot onto the field during the team's entrance.

I had the privilege of meeting not only Matt, the current motorcycle captain, but also his predecessor, Doug. These two men represented different eras of the same cherished tradition, and their pride in their role was evident as they shared stories about their experiences. The opportunity to take photos with both of them, standing beside the famous motorcycle, felt like accessing a special piece of Oregon football history. This chance encounter, following the band's surprise performance and our final "down" shot, exemplified how Oregon football traditions, both old and new, weave together to create an unforgettable game day experience.

By 3:15 p.m., I returned to Jason's tailgate for a brief reunion before heading to Autzen Stadium with him and his wife, Laura. The walk to the stadium was electric: thousands of fans converging, creating a sea of green and yellow with patches of Ohio State scarlet interspersed. The energy heightened with each step as we approached the venue.

Autzen Stadium revealed itself as a masterpiece of college football architecture; it was a single-tier, intimate fifty-four-thousand-seat bowl where every seat promised an excellent view. My location in section 26, row 76, seat 29, offered a perfect vantage point of both the field and the stadium's natural surroundings. What made Autzen truly special was its setting: a variety of tall, majestic deciduous trees in their full autumn splendor created a stunning natural backdrop behind the endzone video scoreboards. Beyond the trees, the mountains loomed in the distance, their silhouettes adding another layer of grandeur to an already impressive scene. The combination of natural beauty and athletic infrastructure created a stadium atmosphere unlike any other in college football.

While Ohio State fans populated my immediate row, the surrounding sections were predominantly Oregon faithful, creating an interesting dynamic of friendly rivalry banter. At precisely 4:29 p.m., the pregame festivities reached their crescendo. The Ohio State team's entrance was met with a thunderous chorus of boos from the home crowd, but what followed was pure Oregon magic. The opposite endzone transformed into a theatrical stage; the Oregon band split into two formations, creating a corridor of sound and pageantry. Suddenly, white smoke billowed across the field, and the familiar roar of that green and black Harley Davidson motorcycle—the same one I'd admired earlier—echoed throughout the stadium. The bike emerged from the smoke, gracefully carrying the Duck mascot down the field. Behind them, the team charged forward while cheerleaders hoisted individual flags that spelled out D-U-C-K-S, creating a moving tapestry of school pride. The choreography of it all—the smoke, the motorcycle, the band, the team, and the flags—captured everything special about college football traditions. As the last flag passed by, my excitement was at its highest as the national anthem completed. It's gametime!

The first half was a masterclass in offensive football, with both powerhouse programs trading explosive plays through the air and on special teams. The back-and-forth battle had the crowd on edge throughout, with Oregon taking a razor-thin 22–21 lead into halftime. But it was the start of the third quarter when Autzen Stadium provided its most breathtaking moment: as the sun began its descent, it painted the sky in brilliant hues that seemed to celebrate the occasion. The setting sun cast its golden light across the autumn trees and distant mountains, creating a majestic backdrop that perfectly framed this top-three matchup. This natural light show only amplified the electric atmosphere inside the stadium, where every play was met with deafening reactions from both fan bases.

The second half maintained the intensity of the first, with neither team able to create significant separation. The energy in Autzen never wavered; each first down was celebrated like a touchdown; each defensive stop cheered like a game-winning play. As the fourth quarter wound down, Ohio State had one final chance, needing only to get into field goal range to steal the victory. The tension was unbearable as the Buckeyes' quarterback scrambled on the final play, but time expired before he could advance the ball far enough, securing Oregon's thrilling 32–31 victory.

What followed was pure euphoria. Thousands of Oregon faithful poured onto the field in a sea of green and yellow, celebrating a victory that felt like more than just a regular season win. The field storming lasted over twenty minutes, and I remained in my seat, soaking in every moment of the celebration while also taking advantage of the chance to claim an abandoned GRASS IS DAMN GREEN IN EUGENE souvenir cup. The party continued well after the final whistle. High-fives between a sea of green and yellow dressed strangers turned into hugs along with the sheer volume of various cheering echoed through the stadium's bowl. This wasn't just a game; it was a spectacle that lived up to its top-three billing, delivering a finish worthy of the stunning venue and passionate crowd.

True to Jason's warning, post-game traffic transformed Eugene into a sea of barely moving vehicles. Rather than fight it, I returned to his tailgate where we spent the next couple of hours reliving not just the thrilling finish but the entire magical day. As other fans shared their favorite moments from the game, I found myself appreciating how this visit had delivered everything I could have hoped for and more: from the campus tour to the multiple tailgate experiences, from meeting remarkable people to witnessing one of college football's most exciting games of the season.

The drive back to Portland stretched to nearly three hours, but I hardly minded. The time allowed me to mentally catalog every moment of this extraordinary day. By the time I reached my hotel, exhaustion had set in, but it was the satisfying kind that comes from experiencing something truly special.

As I settled into my Sunday flight home, I couldn't help but feel that Eugene had given me one of the most complete college football experiences of my journey so far. The combination of natural beauty, passionate fans, multiple welcoming tailgate communities, and an instant classic of a game had set a new standard for my bucket list adventure. Eugene owed me nothing—it had delivered in every possible way.

Yet even as I savored the Oregon experience, anticipation was already building for Week Eight. Waiting for me back in Austin was another potentially epic matchup: the Georgia Bulldogs were coming to town to take on the Texas Longhorns. The prospect of another clash between ranked teams, this time on my home turf, had me buzzing with excitement. The beauty of this bucket list journey was that even after experiencing something as special as Eugene, there was always another promising chapter just around the corner.

#5 GEORGIA AT #1 TEXAS

Week Eight of my bucket list journey took an unexpected but delightful turn. Initially, I had been considering several compelling matchups: Alabama versus Tennessee in a powerful SEC showdown, Kentucky at Florida, and Kansas State versus West Virginia. The West Virginia option was particularly intriguing as I'd never visited the state and was excited about seeing the mountains, though the travel logistics proved challenging. The lodging situations for both the Tennessee game and the Florida game in "the swamp" were prohibitively expensive.

During a late August conversation with my daughter Kennedy, a University of Texas student, everything changed. As I explained my various planned weeks and which games my wife and daughter Lauryn would attend, Kennedy suggested something unexpected: "Dad, what do you think about going to the Texas-Georgia game?" Although my original intention was to visit different cities for each game, I realized that staying in Austin for one game would still technically qualify for the bucket list criteria. The prospect of spending time with Kennedy, even if she'd be seated in the student section, excited me: we could take pictures and videos together before the game.

On September 8th, nearly six weeks before the October 19th game, I made the decision to purchase my ticket for the Texas-Georgia matchup. At the time of purchase, both teams were predicted to be national championship contenders, but I couldn't have anticipated just how significant this game would become. Texas was riding high early in the season, showing promise of reaching the top ranking, while Georgia was maintaining their dominant form from previous seasons. The ticket price of $450 reflected the game's magnitude, but the opportunity to share a gameday experience with Kennedy at my alma mater made it worthwhile. The fact that I wouldn't need additional lodging or airfare, given my Round Rock residence (suburb of Austin), helped justify the ticket cost.

On game day, I started recording my traditional video log around 9:40 a.m. as I prepared for my familiar thirty-five-minute drive from Round Rock to the University of Texas at Austin campus. My excitement was building not just because ESPN College GameDay had already begun broadcasting but because I could feel the energy building across network news and local affiliates about this matchup. The drive down Mopac was filled with cars displaying both Longhorn and Bulldog flags, creating a visual preview of the clash to come.

I strategically chose to park in the West Campus area around 10:30 a.m., knowing this would give me time to catch the final segments of GameDay while waiting to meet Kennedy later. The area was already buzzing with activity: tailgate setups were beginning to emerge at some of the local bar parking lots, and the streets were filling with fans making their way toward the GameDay set. Georgia's fans had traveled well, their red and black attire creating distinct patches among the dominant burnt orange crowd.

After parking, I made my way toward the University of Texas South Mall. This space, selected for the GameDay telecast, sits below the majestic 307-foot-tall UT Tower, one of the most recognizable symbols of higher education in Texas. The South Mall features an expansive green lawn, lined with shade providing oak trees with six red-topped limestone academic buildings—three on each side. A massive Texas state flag elegantly draped the lower portion of the tower's façade, its bold red, white, and blue colors adding to the sense of the occasion. This iconic setting, with its blend of well-placed architectural beauty, created the perfect atmosphere for the morning telecast.

While this marked my fourth College GameDay experience during my fourteen-week bucket list journey, I still wanted to absorb the unique energy each host city brought to the show. With about fifteen minutes remaining in the broadcast, I merged into the crowd of sign-waving fans, capturing videos and photos of the electric atmosphere.

The crowd's energy reached its peak when the GameDay crew made their game predictions. As each commentator picked Texas to win, the gathering of thousands erupted in cheers, punctuated by the powerful blast of the Texas cannon. Even the Georgia fans present, including Jacob and Ryan (whom I met and took selfies with), maintained their respectful demeanor despite the broadcast teams' unanimous picks against the Bulldogs. As we chatted, I shared my bucket list journey, prompting Jacob to say, "I've never met someone who has a bucket list, but if I were to make one, it would have to be as cool as yours!" Ryan nodded in agreement, clearly impressed. These early morning interactions, with fellow football fans set the tone for what would become an unforgettable day on the Forty Acres – an often used moniker of the UT campus to reflect its original size.

The afternoon unfolded like a carefully orchestrated reunion. I spent the morning revisiting my past in the Texas Union, where memories of my student work days came flooding back in the video game room, bowling center, and pool hall. But the day's highlight arrived after 1 p.m. when Kennedy met me outside at the Union's entrance staircase. It was an emotional moment I'll never forget. We immediately captured the moment on video, both of us beaming in our matching burnt orange UT attire. I had on my cap and shirt, Kennedy in her boots, jean skirt with UT colored top as we were preparing to attend our first football game together.

Our first stop was the GameDay bus, which was still parked near the UT Tower even though the broadcast had ended hours earlier. We took advantage of the perfect photo opportunity, capturing several shots that would memorialize our first Texas game day together. Though the GameDay set was being dismantled, the energy around campus remained electric, with fans still milling about the area taking their own photos.

With Kennedy scheduled to meet her girlfriends around 3 p.m., we made the most of our time together. We headed toward the adjacent streets where I knew the prime tailgating spots would be located. I had reached out to my former co-worker Jeff earlier, who confirmed his regular crew—including Charlie, Benny, and Madeline—would be at their usual tailgate spot and welcomed me and Kennedy. But before heading there, Kennedy and I took a leisurely stroll up and down San Jacinto Boulevard, immersing ourselves in the gameday atmosphere. Various tailgate hosts graciously offered us snacks and drinks, exemplifying the hospitality that makes college football so special.

Around 2:00 p.m., we found Charlie's tailgate spot along the adjacent street. Charlie, Benny, and Madeline were in the midst of their setup preparations, with portable tents providing shade and tables being arranged for the feast to come. As I introduced Kennedy to the group, Charlie's face lit up with recognition: even though years had passed since our last encounter, the connection from countless previous tailgates remained strong.

The elaborate setup was still taking shape, with Charlie informing us that their full spread of food—including tamales, tacos and brisket—would be ready closer to 3 p.m. The aroma of meat smoking in their smoker already filled the air, promising the delicious feast to come. Coolers lined the perimeter, stocked with both alcoholic and non-alcoholic beverages, and they graciously offered us water to combat the warm Texas afternoon.

While the main food wasn't quite ready, they had already set out some appetizers, including chips and dips. Charlie, a seasoned tailgating veteran, was organizing the space with the precision that comes from years of gameday experience. During our brief visit, I caught Kennedy observing the well-orchestrated setup with fascination—having only experienced game days with her student friends in the stands, this pregame ritual with its elaborate tents, grills, and coordinated festivities was an entirely new side of Texas football culture for her.

The reunion with Charlie and the crew provided a perfect bridge between my past Texas football experiences and this new chapter of sharing the tradition with Kennedy. Though our visit was brief, as we wanted to explore Bevo Boulevard, the warmth of their welcome and Charlie's invitation to return later for food demonstrated the enduring spirit of Texas tailgating community.

After our initial stop at Charlie's tailgate, Kennedy and I made our way toward Bevo Boulevard, the vibrant pregame festival that transforms San Jacinto Boulevard into a Longhorn celebration. Located just outside Darrell K. Royal-Texas Memorial Stadium, this relatively new addition to the gameday experience had quickly become a must-visit destination for fans.

The atmosphere was electric as we entered the free festivities. Rows of food trucks lined the street, their various aromas mixing with the excitement in the air. Live radio broadcasts were taking place from designated stations, with hosts engaging fans and discussing the upcoming top-five matchup. One of the most eye-catching features was the zip line stretching above the crowd, with adventurous fans soaring overhead to the cheers of onlookers below.

Multiple large television screens were strategically placed throughout the area, broadcasting other college games and adding to the football-saturated environment. Vendors had set up shop selling everything from commemorative t-shirts to gameday accessories, mostly themed around the historic Texas-Georgia matchup. The crowd was a sea of burnt orange, punctuated by pockets of Georgia's red and black.

As we navigated through the festival-like atmosphere, we encountered one of Kennedy's classmates, whose parents had made the journey from Georgia for the game. This chance meeting led to an engaging conversation, during which I shared stories about my bucket list journey. The father, a Georgia alum, nodded thoughtfully and shared, "With our daughters being out of the house on their way to graduating one day, it's these milestone achievements as parents that get you in a position to do something like a bucket list, and I admire you for doing this." They were eager to compare the UT gameday experience to their beloved Athens traditions, having attended countless games at Sanford Stadium. The Georgia family seemed genuinely impressed by the ambitious nature of my fourteen-week football adventure, and we exchanged perspectives on our respective football traditions.

Kennedy and I decided to grab some pizza and drinks, finding a spot to sit and soak in the atmosphere. The time seemed to fly by as we enjoyed our food and the surrounding entertainment, knowing we had until about 3 p.m. before Kennedy needed to meet her friends to line up for the student section.

The experience of sharing this modern Texas tradition with Kennedy, while creating our own new memories, made Bevo Boulevard more than just a pregame celebration. It represented the perfect blend of Texas football's storied past and its evolution into the future, all while allowing us to share a special father-daughter moment in the midst of my bucket list journey.

As 3 p.m. approached, Kennedy and I savored our final moments together on Bevo Boulevard. We took our last round of photos, and she explained which section of the student area she planned to sit in while I shared my seat location in Section 111. Though we wouldn't be able to sit together, there was something special about knowing we'd both be experiencing this historic matchup under the same stadium lights. After one final hug, Kennedy headed off to meet her friends and secure their spots in the student section.

With Kennedy gone, I made my way back to Charlie's tailgate, where the culinary spread was impressive: tacos with perfectly seasoned meat, tender brisket that had been smoking for hours, and an array of sides that showcased true Texas tailgating at its finest. Thirsty – well Tito's vodka with tonic and assorted juices for cocktails, an array of beer options, along with water and sodas were all available. The spread was made complete with sweet treats: cookies and brownies for all to enjoy.

The atmosphere at Charlie's had grown livelier, with more fans gathering around. I found myself sharing my bucket list journey story with several fellow tailgaters at an adjacent spot who were intrigued by my fourteen-week adventure. During these conversations, I met Paul, who was crafting impressive smash burgers on a portable griddle. He was making these burgers for anyone who stopped by, including a Georgia fan named Roger.

My interaction with Roger, decked out in his Georgia red and black, proved particularly memorable. "Welcome to Austin!" I greeted him with a grin, adding playfully, "but just know these Dawgs are going down today!" We shared a laugh before diving into our respective football traditions. I couldn't help but relive the famous standoff between Bevo, UT's live longhorn mascot, and UGA, Georgia's bulldog, at the 2019 Sugar Bowl. "Let's hope our mascots behave today," I laughed, and Roger joined in the laughter, recalling the viral moment. As we chatted further about UT and Georgia football traditions, I mentioned my plans to attend a game in Athens later in the season, specifically the Tennessee game before Thanksgiving weekend. Roger's face lit up as he extended an incredibly gracious offer, inviting me to his tailgate at Legion Pool parking lot as he had a setup for every Georgia home game.

The tailgate reached another level of excitement when my old friend Jeff and his wife, Catie, arrived just after 5 p.m. As we caught up on old times and shared stories of past game days, the energy continued building with kickoff approaching. Our conversation about memorable games of past seasons eventually led to the present-day Longhorns, currently ranked #1 in the nation. Speculation kicked in: Could we be witnessing the dawn of another championship run, like the glory days of 2005? As we talked through this, our excitement for the evening's clash against Georgia intensified. The blend of UT's past, their current success, and anticipation for the game ahead created a perfect prelude to the main event, leaving us eager for kickoff and the potential history we might witness.

Around 5:30 p.m., our group began packing up the tailgate and preparing for the twenty-minute walk to the stadium. The sun was slowly beginning to set, and the excitement among the streams of fans heading toward DKR was intense. This transition from tailgate to stadium marked the end of one phase of game day and the beginning of another, all while carrying the warmth of both old friendships renewed and new connections made.

By 6:00 PM, I had settled into my seat in Section 111, Row 1, Seat 9 in the upper deck. The location proved perfect: no one blocking my view, and I faced both the TEXAS end zone and the massive JumboTron. Just before 6:30 p.m., the pregame festivities began with the Longhorn Band taking the field. As per Longhorn tradition, the band's precision movements spelled out T-E-X-A-S before transitioning into a formation of the letter *T* and finally morphing into the iconic Longhorn symbol. The choreography was flawless, accompanied by the familiar strains of traditional Texas football songs that echoed throughout the stadium.

The national anthem provided one of the evening's most spectacular moments. As the band held their Longhorn formation and the anthem played, a formation of F-16 fighter planes roared overhead in perfect timing. The flyover, combined with a stunning fireworks display, sent chills through the sellout crowd, igniting a wave of cheers that reverberated throughout the stands.

When the Georgia team was introduced and emerged from the tunnel, they were met with a thunderous chorus of boos from the Texas faithful. The Bulldogs, ranked #5, took it in stride as they had surely experienced similar welcomes in other SEC venues. Their entrance was straightforward but carried the confidence of a team that had been in many big-game situations.

The Texas entrance, by contrast, was pure spectacle. The massive video board filled with a hype video as music from AC/DC's track "Hells Bells" pounded through the stadium speakers. The cheerleaders created their traditional "T" formation on the field, splitting apart as the team emerged from the tunnel. The spectacle was enhanced by cheerleaders running ahead of the team, wielding illuminated fire sticks that created trails of orange smoke. Others held individual letters spelling "T-E-X-A-S," while the enormous Longhorn flag led the procession. The roar of the crowd was deafening as the #1 ranked Longhorns took the field.

During the pregame festivities, I struck up a conversation with Patrick, who was there with his wife in the seats next to mine. As we talked about the upcoming matchup, I shared a bit about my journey—how this was week eight of my college football tour. Patrick asked if I was following a specific team and whether I'd seen the Longhorns play anywhere else. I told him I caught them in week two at the Big House in Michigan. He then asked about the upcoming stops for weeks nine through fourteen, and after hearing more, he said, "Man that's bad ass, you should capture these trips online somewhere as folks would love hearing about something like this." At the time, I had no plans of writing a book. I was content sharing stories with friends and family, sending them the occasional video or photo. But when he added, "That makes me want to do something like this when I retire," it really stuck with me. It made me realize how sharing this journey doesn't just spark curiosity—it inspires people to think about their own "what" and "when."

The stadium was a sea of burnt orange, with pockets of Georgia red and black scattered throughout. The energy was off the charts: this wasn't just another game, but a top-five matchup with national championship implications. As both teams finished their warm-ups and the sun began to set over Austin, the stage was set for what promised to be an epic showdown between two of college football's most storied programs.

The first half proved to be a sobering experience for the Texas faithful. Georgia's dominance was methodical and relentless, as they systematically built a 23–0 lead heading into halftime. Their ground game proved particularly effective, with each of their touchdowns coming via the rushing attack. The Bulldogs' defense matched their offense's intensity, stifling Texas's typically explosive offense and silencing the normally boisterous home crowd.

However, the Longhorns showed signs of life as they emerged from the locker room for the third quarter. The team that took the field appeared reinvigorated, and their renewed energy quickly translated to points. Texas mounted an impressive comeback, scoring 15 unanswered points that brought the crowd back to life and injected hope into the stadium. The sequence of scores reminded everyone why Texas had earned their #1 ranking, even if they'd struggled in the first half.

Then, around 9:30 p.m., between the third and fourth quarters, the stadium witnessed something truly spectacular. The lights dimmed, and the night sky above DKR became a canvas for what would prove to be the most impressive drone show I'd ever seen. Hundreds of synchronized drones took to the air, first spelling out LONGHORNS in flowing cursive script with brilliant orange lights. As this display transitioned, another section of the sky illuminated with the word TEXAS in bold lettering.

But the show was just beginning. The drones then reorganized to create a massive Longhorn head that appeared to actually shake in an incredibly lifelike feat of animation. Even more impressively, the digital bovine appeared to blow smoke from its nostrils. The display then transformed again, with the full-sized Longhorn becoming just the face of the mascot. In a stunning sequence, a cannon formed in the background, appearing to fire at the Longhorn head. When the symbolic shot connected, the entire display erupted into a brilliant fireworks show.

The grand finale featured the drones reforming into the iconic "Hook 'em Horns" hand signal, glowing bright orange against the dark Austin sky. The entire stadium stood in awe of the technological masterpiece, momentarily forgetting the tension of the game. Even the Georgia fans around me couldn't help but applaud the spectacular display. In my years of attending sporting events, I had never seen anything quite like it—the perfect marriage of tradition and technology, creating a new kind of gameday magic.

The fourth quarter brought one of the most controversial moments I've witnessed in college football. During a crucial defensive stand, Texas appeared to make a game-changing interception, only to have it nullified by a questionable pass interference call. The penalty sparked immediate outrage throughout DKR, and the situation quickly escalated. Frustrated fans began throwing water bottles onto the field, a classless display that brought the game to a halt as officials cleared the field for safety.

In an unprecedented turn of events that I'd never seen in all my years of watching football, the officials actually reviewed the play and overturned the pass interference call, allowing the interception to stand. This rare reversal drew a thunderous roar from the crowd, momentarily restoring hope for a Texas comeback. However, the elation would prove short-lived.

Despite Texas intercepting Georgia's quarterback Carson Beck three times throughout the game, the Bulldogs' ground game proved too powerful to overcome. Georgia methodically controlled the clock and field position, scoring the only touchdown of the fourth quarter to secure a 30–15 victory. All three of Georgia's touchdowns came on the ground, demonstrating their physical dominance at the line of scrimmage.

Texas's performance told a tale of two halves—completely shut out in the first half at 23–0, then showing signs of life with fifteen unanswered points in the third quarter. However, their inability to capitalize on the three interceptions and a series of untimely penalties ultimately proved costly. The Bulldogs showed why they were a perennial powerhouse, maintaining their composure even when Texas threatened to make it a game.

The stadium began to empty gradually, but I remained in my seat for about forty-five minutes after the final whistle, watching as the hundred-thousand-plus fans slowly filtered out. Before leaving, I made sure to grab my Texas Longhorn souvenir cup, adding another memento to my growing collection from the bucket list journey. The thirty-five-minute walk back to my car provided time to reflect on a game that, while disappointing in outcome, had delivered plenty of memorable moments both on and off the field.

Georgia had proven why they were consistently among the nation's elite programs, while Texas showed both their potential and the areas where they still needed to grow to compete at the highest level. The final score of 30–15 reflected Georgia's overall dominance but didn't tell the full story of Texas's resilience in the second half or the electric atmosphere that had permeated the entire day.

As I drove back to Round Rock that night, this game felt distinctly different from my previous bucket list experiences. While the outcome wasn't what Texas fans had hoped for, the day had delivered something far more valuable than just a football game. The opportunity to share gameday traditions with Kennedy, even if only for a few pregame hours, had made the $450 ticket price seem insignificant compared to the memories we'd created.

Each moment replayed in my mind: Kennedy's excited arrival at the Union, our exploration of Bevo Boulevard together, the chance encounters with friendly Georgia fans, the spectacular drone show, and even the controversial moments that kept fans on the edge of their seats. The day had perfectly bridged my past experiences as a Texas student with Kennedy's present journey at UT.

Looking ahead to Week Nine, my thoughts began turning to Ohio State. However, this Texas game would clearly stand out in my journey. While other weeks focused on discovering new venues and traditions, this one had been about coming home: not just to my alma mater but to the fundamental reason why college football means so much to so many people. It's about family, tradition, and the connections that span generations.

Charlie's tailgate hospitality, the Georgia fans who welcomed me to their future home game, and even Patrick's friendly conversation in the stands: all exemplified why I had undertaken this fourteen-week adventure. As I pulled into my driveway in Round Rock, I couldn't help but smile, knowing that while the scoreboard showed a loss, the day had been an absolute win in every way that truly mattered.

The prospect of Ohio State's historic Horseshoe awaited in Week Nine, but for now, I savored this perfect blend of past and present, father and daughter, tradition and innovation. Sometimes the most meaningful stops on a bucket list journey are the ones that bring you back home, reminding you why you started the journey in the first place.

NEBRASKA AT #4 OHIO STATE

W eek Nine of the bucket list was a no-brainer. I knew I wanted to go to Columbus, Ohio, and take on a game at *THE* Ohio State to check out the Buckeyes. They would be hosting the Nebraska Cornhuskers for this matchup. For Week Nine, I flew into Columbus on Friday, October 25th. The game was scheduled for the 26th, a noon game—an early kickoff—and I would head home on Sunday.

My planning for Week Nine started and came to completion on July 19th. I bought my airfare, confirmed my Airbnb, rental car, and got my game ticket. The football rich history of The Ohio State University made it a must-see destination on my list. I heard about the mystique of the electric atmosphere of a fall football Saturday in Big 10 country and I wanted the opportunity to take it all in. Anticipating seeing a sea of fans dressed in scarlet and gray pack one of college football's most iconic venues, speaks to the program's legacy of winning eight national championships. Growing up I watched the

Buckeyes on TV, from their thrilling bowl game appearances to the intensity of their annual showdowns with rival Michigan: a rivalry many consider one of the greatest in all of college sports.

After arriving mid-to-late afternoon on Friday, I picked up my rental car and headed to my Airbnb in Grove City, Ohio, which I had chosen for its convenient location about twelve miles from campus. My first stop was the Grove City Walmart, where I bought an Ohio State hat to complement the red t-shirt I'd brought for the game. I planned to pair these with a light jacket, anticipating temperatures starting in the mid-40s.

After checking into my Airbnb, I decided to have dinner at Windward Passage, a highly rated restaurant where I was able to get a seat at the bar despite the growing crowd. (It's usually pretty easy to get a spot at a crowded restaurant with a party of one.) Following my delicious meal around 7 p.m., I headed toward campus, which was bustling with activity due to it being homecoming weekend. The parade was just wrapping up, and both Nebraska and Ohio State fans filled the streets. I used this time to scout the area and plan my parking strategy for game day, eventually finding a Starbucks about a mile and a half from the stadium that would serve as my morning parking spot.

On my drive back into Grove City around 8 p.m., I discovered a lively atmosphere of the Heart of Grove City Food Truck Festival and Shop taking place just three blocks from my Airbnb in the town center. The event perfectly captured the charm of small town Ohio, with local shops keeping their doors open late while food trucks lined the streets offering everything from gourmet tacos to grilled cheese sandwiches. I couldn't resist ordering the loaded fries, piled high with cheese and bacon, though I managed to show restraint by passing on one of the dessert truck's tempting ice creams. As live music filled the air and families enjoyed moving around the venue, I continued enjoying the warm community atmosphere before heading back for a well-deserved rest as I would need to start early in the morning.

Saturday morning began at 5:30 a.m. After showering and recording my customary video describing my location and plans, I drove to the previously scouted Starbucks around 6 a.m. After getting coffee and a pastry, I took an Uber to the Blackwell Inn, a hotel nestled right on Ohio State's campus. The lobby and surrounding areas were already buzzing with excitement by 7 a.m., as fans from both schools gathered in small groups, enjoying their morning coffee and sharing predictions for the day ahead. The scene was predominantly colors of scarlet and gray, though patches of Nebraska red were sprinkled throughout. The gameday energy suddenly intensified when someone shouted "OH!" which was immediately answered by a thunderous "IO!" from the Buckeye faithful: a cherished call-and-response tradition that echoed through the lobby. Ohio State fans were out in particularly strong numbers, their enthusiasm amplified by the special energy of homecoming weekend. I found a comfortable spot to enjoy the mingling of Buckeye families reunited and visiting Husker fans.

Around 8:45 a.m., I made my way toward the Fox Big Noon Kickoff show setup located just outside Ohio Stadium, reminiscent of my experience at the Texas-Michigan game. En route, I encountered one of Ohio State's notable superfans, Buck I Guy: complete with his signature cowboy hat and Ohio State cape, bandana covering his nose and chin and signature white sunglasses. I managed to get a selfie with this television fixture before proceeding to the Fox setup, where a DJ was providing entertainment. I took advantage of photo opportunities with a Greetings from Columbus sign and a huge inflatable Brutus, the Ohio State mascot.

I stayed at the Big Noon Kickoff till about 9:30 or so, and then decided I wanted to walk over from the setup a little bit closer to some of the stadium parking lots to see what the tailgate situation was, as it was now about two and a half hours before kickoff. I know that the morning tailgate sessions are a little different than the afternoon or late game kickoffs due to the fact that it's typically a breakfast type of environment—people were just waking up. It's still a good vibe, but it's a different vibe.

The first person I encountered during my tailgating exploration was Jason, who immediately caught my attention with his distinctive gameday attire: an oversized Ohio State hat paired with eye-catching red- and white-striped overalls. His tailgate setup was among the most impressive I'd seen, positioned perfectly in the parking lot with an elaborate spread that would make any foodie envious.

When I approached and introduced myself, explaining my fourteen-week college football bucket list journey, Jason's eyes lit up with genuine enthusiasm as he said, "Come on in, let's get you something to eat and I want to hear about this." His tailgate spread was a culinary masterpiece: a full-fledged shrimp and crab boil, savory breakfast tacos loaded with fresh ingredients, and homemade meatballs. Bourbon-infused warm apple cider provided just the right amount of warmth for the crisp October morning.

What stood out most was how Jason and his friends reacted to my bucket list story. They weren't just being nice; they were completely hooked by the concept. Jason's friends, a mix of longtime Ohio State season ticket holders and co-workers, began peppering me with questions about my experiences. I shared stories about the incredible drone show lighting up the Austin night sky before a Texas game, and how Oregon's campus in Eugene took my breath away with its pristine beauty nestled against the mountains. At each stop, I'd encountered the same warm welcome from tailgate hosts who, just like this crew, had welcomed me into their pregame celebrations.

Their energy was through the roof as they discussed among themselves how they could replicate something similar. This wasn't just small talk; they were truly fired up to create their own college football pilgrimage. I captured the whole interaction on video, and they perfectly summed up their newfound inspiration by closing with an enthusiastic "we're doing it, we're doing it!"

The group's hospitality was remarkable as they insisted I try everything they had prepared, treating me like a longtime friend rather than a stranger who had wandered into their tailgate.

This interaction exemplified what makes college football culture so special: the way complete strangers can bond over a shared love of the game and inspire each other to pursue new adventures. As I left Jason's tailgate, with a full belly and warm heart, I couldn't help but think that this was exactly the kind of meaningful connection I had hoped to make when planning this bucket list journey.

As I moved onto the next tailgate setup in the same parking lot, I walked up and introduced myself with my normal bucket list intro: "Hi, I'm Anthony from Austin. I'm doing a fourteen-week bucket list where I'm going to a different college game in a different city for the entire season." This was said to four wonderful ladies from northeast Ohio, Dana, Jen, Kristin, and Josie, who were all rocking sunglasses and slightly bundled up in fall weather scarlet and gray . After their cheerful chorus of "Welcome to Columbus," Dana said, "You've got the coolest wife" (I couldn't agree more). She shared her thoughts on how great it was that my wife had fully embraced my bucket list journey, and they all agreed the trips were an awesome idea.

Not only were they affiliated with a fruit farm (Patterson Fruit Farm), but also a bakery. The ladies were really cool, and I was able to dialogue with them for probably ten to fifteen minutes while enjoying some of their apple cider (sorry Jason, theirs was better!), which was absolutely awesome, and the maple bacon donut was off the chain.

It turns out that Kristin had been a longtime Cleveland Browns fan but had lost her allegiance as they continued to have an underwhelming team. However, she's definitely a diehard Ohio State Buckeyes fan that tries to make every home tailgate that she could. I was so glad I was able to stop by and enjoy some additional breakfast with them as their food and drinks were delicious.

As I continued moving around the parking lot, I was drawn to a tent hosted by Crafted Culture Brewing Company, central Ohio's first Black-owned brewery. There I met John, one of the company reps, who wanted me to sample their Pineapple Krunk Juice IPA. The beers tropical profile and balanced flavor made it perfect for a few game day sips. Even though I was being careful with alcohol consumption before the noon game, the experience of meeting John and learning about his company added another rich layer to my Columbus gameday experience. It was these kinds of unexpected encounters—meeting local business owners who are passionate about their craft and their community—that made each stop on my bucket list journey unique and memorable.

Around 10:15, the gameday atmosphere shifted as fans began congregating near the iconic Archie Griffin statue for one of Ohio State's cherished traditions: welcoming the team to the stadium. The area around the statue became a sea of scarlet and gray as fans positioned themselves along the path where the team would soon make their entrance. The energy was electric, with the anticipation building among the gathered crowd.

The Archie Griffin statue served as more than just a meeting point: it stood as a symbol of Ohio State's rich football heritage, honoring the only two-time Heisman Trophy winner in college football history. I took a moment to capture some photos of this historic landmark, watching as families and students posed for their own pictures, creating their gameday memories.

This pregame ritual highlighted how Ohio State football transcends being just a sport: it's a unifying force that brings together thousands of people from different backgrounds, all sharing in the tradition and pageantry of college football. Standing there among the enthusiastic fans, I could feel why this tradition meant so much to the Ohio State faithful and why it had become such an integral part of the gameday experience.

Clad in matching gray sweatsuits and mostly wearing headphones, the players made their way to the stadium with a quiet business-like focus. The energy around the statue and team entrance area would set the tone for the rest of the day's festivities, marking the transition from tailgating and pregame celebrations to the serious business of Big Ten football. It was these kinds of traditions, these moments of communal anticipation and celebration, that made my bucket list journey so special and Ohio State's gameday experience unique.

At 10:30 a.m., I made my way into the historic Ohio Stadium, famously known as "The Horseshoe" due to its original open-ended, U-shaped design when it first opened in 1922. My seat location— Section 14A, Row 26, Seat 13—positioned me perfectly in the curve of the Horseshoe's U-shape, offering an excellent vantage point of both the field and the overall stadium atmosphere. The morning dew still clung to the seats, a reminder of the crisp fall morning, though I knew the combination of the emerging sun and the heat of 102,000-plus fans would soon take care of that.

As I explored the stadium's concourse, I couldn't help but be struck by the venue's architectural charm, which was inspired by the university's neoclassical style. The concrete columns and arches, weathered by nearly a century of Ohio football history, told their own story.

During my exploration, I encountered one of Ohio State's most recognizable superfans: "Big Nut." He was impossible to miss with his elaborate gameday appearance: face meticulously painted in scarlet and gray, adorned with countless Ohio State beads and decorations, embodying the passionate spirit of Buckeye fandom. Big Nut wasn't just dressed for the occasion; he was a walking tribute to Ohio State football tradition.

What made the encounter particularly special was Big Nut's welcoming nature. Despite his celebrity status among Ohio State fans (he's regularly featured on national television broadcasts), he was incredibly approachable and genuine. He happily posed for photos, even letting me hold his prized Brutus doll for some pictures.

The interaction with Big Nut exemplified what makes college football special: how the most devoted fans become part of the institution itself, adding their own chapter to the university's rich tradition. Here was someone who had transformed his passion for Ohio State football into a persona that brought joy to countless other fans, becoming as much a part of the gameday experience as the stadium itself.

This early entry gave me the opportunity to truly absorb the magnitude of Ohio Stadium before it filled to capacity. Watching the gradual transformation from an empty concrete bowl to a roaring sea of scarlet and gray would be one of the day's highlights, and I was grateful to experience every moment of it.

Around 11:30 a.m., as the stadium began filling with anticipation for kickoff, I met the couple who would add unexpected depth to my gameday experience. Val and Butch settled into their seats to my right, and what began as casual gameday small talk evolved into one of the most meaningful interactions of my entire bucket list journey.

When I shared the story of my fourteen-week college football journey, their reaction was different from the typical "that's really cool" or "wow" responses I usually received. Butch, in particular, was really fired up by my discussion. His eyes lit up behind his sunglasses with excitement as he absorbed every detail of my adventures, asking thoughtful questions about the different venues I'd visited and the traditions I'd experienced.

Without hesitation, he turned to Val and declared with conviction that they would attend every Ohio State away game the following season as this was something that he had always wanted to do. It wasn't just idle talk; you could hear the determination in his voice, as if my story had unlocked a sense of urgency to pursue their own adventures while they still could.

What made this interaction particularly poignant was Val's quiet revelation about their own situation. She confided that Butch's vision was progressively deteriorating, a reality that had been weighing heavily on them both. This disclosure added profound context to Butch's enthusiastic response to my bucket list story.

The conversation deepened when they proudly shared that their grandson was a walk-on receiver for Ohio State, where he's a member of the team but without an athletic scholarship. Their faces beamed with pride as they spoke about his journey to join the team, adding another layer to their deep connection with Buckeye football.

What struck me most about Val and Butch was how my simple story had sparked something deeper within them. Here was a couple facing their own challenges, yet finding inspiration to embrace new adventures rather than retreat from them.

This encounter embodied something I hadn't anticipated when planning my bucket list journey: how sharing my adventure could inspire others to create their own. What started as a personal quest to experience college football's greatest venues had become something more meaningful, serving as a catalyst for others to pursue their dreams, even in the face of personal challenges. Val and Butch's story became a powerful reminder that these stadium visits weren't just about the games; they were about the connections made and the lives touched along the way.

As 11:45 a.m. approached, the energy within Ohio Stadium reached a new level of intensity. The massive venue was transforming from a historic structure into a living, breathing entity as scarlet and gray-clad fans filled every available space. The atmosphere was electric with anticipation for one of college football's most revered traditions.

The Ohio State University Marching Band, known as "The Best Damn Band in the Land," gathered in formation at the end zone nestled within the U-shape of the horseshoe. Their presence alone caused a stir among the crowd, as everyone knew what was coming. The band's entrance was a spectacle in itself, led by the head drum major in his traditional uniform, complete with the tall bearskin hat that has become synonymous with Ohio State football.

What happened next was a display of precision and tradition that left me awestruck. As the band marched onto the field, the drum major performed one of the most iconic moves in college football: stopping at the thirty-five-yard line and executing a deep backbend until the plume of his bearskin hat touched the Buckeye logo on the field. The crowd erupted in cheers at this display of flexibility and showmanship, a tradition that has become one of the most photographed moments of any Ohio State game.

In a particularly touching display of sportsmanship that I hadn't expected, the band transitioned into a formation honoring their opponents. As the stadium announcer introduced the day's matchup against the Nebraska Cornhuskers, the band precisely maneuvered to form a perfect *N:* Nebraska's iconic logo. This gesture of respect toward the visiting team demonstrated a level of class that impressed me, especially given the intense rivalries of Big Ten football.

The stadium was now nearly full, with fans standing shoulder to shoulder in the aisles and steady streams of people still filing in through every entrance. The atmosphere was building toward what everyone knew would be the main event: the famous "Script Ohio." The anticipation was evident as the clock ticked toward 11:57, when one of college football's most celebrated traditions would begin. The precision with which the band members maneuvered was mesmerizing, each step carefully choreographed as they weaved across the field creating the cursive letters. The formation began with a single drum major leading the winding procession of percussion, slowly but deliberately forming each letter of "Ohio" in an elegant cursive script. The crowd's energy built with each letter formed, but everyone knew the best was yet to come. As the formation neared completion, all eyes focused on a single sousaphone player who would finish off the script and "dot the i" in an elegantly bowing fashion, which was met with a unison of cheers from the Buckeye faithful.

As kickoff approached, Val gently tapped my shoulder and motioned toward my binoculars. "You'll want to see this," she said with a knowing smile, directing my attention to the student section. She explained a unique Ohio State tradition I hadn't known about. During kickoff, students would remove one shoe and wave it in the air, a quirky ritual that made perfect sense given the stadium's "Horseshoe" nickname. Sure enough, as the teams lined up for kickoff, hundreds of shoes were suddenly hoisted skyward, creating an oddly beautiful sight that perfectly captured the peculiar charm of college football traditions.

The first half of football that followed was, to be honest, less impressive than the pregame festivities. Despite Ohio State being ranked #4 in the country, their performance seemed sluggish and uninspired. They managed to take a 14–6 lead into halftime, but the execution wasn't what you'd expect from a top-five team. The usually electric atmosphere in the Horseshoe felt somewhat subdued, with Buckeye fans seeming more anxious than excited. The team's performance had the crowd murmuring with concern rather than cheering with their usual gusto.

Throughout the game, we shared observations and commentary, celebrating good plays and groaning at setbacks together. Their knowledge of Ohio State football added rich context to the game unfolding before us. I learned from Val, that although her grandson was a walk-on member of the football team, the team does not allow walkons to attend away games. But more than just these conversations, their presence transformed what would have been just another stadium visit into a deeply personal experience.

However, what the first half lacked in excitement, the halftime show more than made up for with a spectacular tribute to Frank

Sinatra. While I wouldn't consider myself a Sinatra fan, the Ohio State Marching Band's performance was nothing short of extraordinary. They opened by spelling "Sinatra" in perfect cursive formation, but that was just the beginning. What followed was a masterclass in precision marching and creative choreography.

The band transformed themselves into the shapes of a man and woman on the field, then ingeniously used other band members to create the illusion of the male figure rolling dice toward the female figure. The complexity and execution of these formations were astounding: it was like watching a living, breathing animation created by hundreds of musicians in perfect synchronization.

The show's highlight came when the band formed an airplane on the field. This wasn't just a static formation. They also created the illusion of the plane taking off, complete with what appeared to be jet exhaust trailing behind it, all formed by band members in constant, precise motion. The level of coordination required to pull this off was mind-boggling. This was followed by a heart shaped formation and two wine glasses that toasted each other. What an amazing spectacle of choreography!

As the show reached its finale with "My Way," the band created yet another innovative display. They spelled out M-Y W-A-Y while incorporating delicate details like eyelashes above the text: a level of intricacy that seemed almost impossible for a marching band to achieve. The performance concluded with the formation of two top hats as they played "New York, New York," providing a perfect bookend to their Sinatra tribute.

The halftime show served as a powerful reminder of why they call themselves "The Best Damn Band in the Land." Even as someone who had seen many college halftime shows during my bucket list journey, this performance stood apart. The precision, creativity, and sheer ambition of the show was unlike anything I'd witnessed before. It was a perfect example of how Ohio State's gameday experience extends far beyond just the football being played on the field.

The contrast between the somewhat lackluster first half of football and the spectacular halftime show created an interesting dynamic. While the team might not have been performing at their peak, the band certainly was, providing a reminder that college football Saturdays are about much more than just the game itself.

The second half of the game brought the drama that the first half had lacked. The tension in the Horseshoe reached its peak in the fourth quarter when Nebraska, playing the role of spoiler, took a shocking 17–14 lead. The stadium's energy shifted dramatically; you could feel the collective anxiety of 104,000 fans who hadn't anticipated such a close contest against an unranked opponent. Yet this moment of adversity seemed to finally wake up the fourth-ranked Buckeyes.

Ohio State responded with a renewed sense of urgency, mounting a crucial drive that resulted in a touchdown to retake the lead 21–17. The stadium erupted with a mixture of relief and celebration as the Buckeyes managed to avoid what would have been a devastating upset. The defense held firm in the final minutes, preserving the victory and allowing the nervous energy in the stadium to finally release into celebration.

After the final whistle, I remained in my seat for about thirty-five minutes, letting the capacity crowd filter out while taking in the final moments of my visit to the Horseshoe. The late afternoon sun cast long shadows across the field, and the autumn air had warmed to a comfortable mid-60s—perfect football weather. As the stands emptied, I collected a souvenir cup to add to my growing collection from each stadium visited, a small but meaningful memento of my time in Columbus.

Around 4 p.m., I made my way out of the stadium and spent some time walking around the campus. The postgame atmosphere was festive despite the closer-than-expected score, with fans still celebrating on the beautiful Ohio State grounds. As I walked back toward my car, I found myself reflecting on what made this Week Nine experience so special.

While early kickoff games often lack the same energy as afternoon or evening contests, this visit had proved different. The connections I'd made—from the welcoming tailgate hosts to the meaningful interaction with Butch and Val—had added unexpected depth to my journey. What struck me most was how my personal bucket list quest had managed to inspire others, particularly Butch and Val, to pursue their own adventures. This wasn't something I had anticipated when planning this journey, but it had become one of its most rewarding aspects.

The whole experience—from the Grove City food truck festival on Friday night to the iconic Script Ohio formation, and from the spectacular halftime show to the dramatic game finish—had come together to create another unforgettable chapter in my bucket list journey. Each week seemed to offer its own unique flavor of college football culture, and Columbus had certainly delivered its own special blend of tradition, pageantry, and human connection.

As I headed back to my Grove City Airbnb for one last night before my Sunday morning departure, my thoughts were already drifting to Week Ten in Jackson, Mississippi, where my wife would be joining me. But for now, I savored the satisfaction of another successful stadium visit, another set of memories made, and another reminder of why college football Saturdays are so special.

Week Nine had reinforced what I had been learning throughout this journey: while the games themselves are important, it's the people you meet, the traditions you experience, and the connections you make that truly make college football culture unique. The Horseshoe had lived up to its reputation, not just as a historic venue, but as a place where lasting memories are made and where the spirit of college football thrives in its purest form.

ARKANSAS PINE BLUFF AT JACKSON STATE

T he planning for my Week Ten venture to Jackson State University's homecoming game against Arkansas Pine Bluff began during a July 4th pool party. My friend Mitch, a Jackson State alum who attended homecoming every year, encouraged me to include this HBCU (Historically Black Colleges and Universities) experience in my fourteen-week bucket list journey. The suggestion particularly resonated with me since Jackson, Mississippi, was my mother's birthplace.

My connection to Jackson runs deep through childhood memories of regular visits to see my maternal grandparents. The eight-hour drives from Houston were an adventure in themselves. Mom would often pack homemade fried chicken, and we'd make our routine stop in Crowley, Louisiana, for gas. Sometimes, when we were younger and couldn't stop, we'd have to make do with an old Maxwell House coffee can for bathroom emergencies.

As my mother and maternal grandparents are deceased, Grandma's house held special memories. It faced westbound on a modest street, though she always sat in her northward-facing window, watching for our arrival. She would inevitably spot our car turning onto her street and hurry down her back stairway to greet us with excitement in the driveway. The house itself was a classic shotgun-style home: you entered through front stairs into the living room, which led to the kitchen and finally to a back living room with stairs to the back porch and detached garage. Three bedrooms and one bathroom made for interesting logistics when we got together with other cousins and relatives.

Life was simpler then. The house had just one television without cable service, leaving us with limited channel options in the 70s and 80s. But that hardly mattered; we spent our time talking and enjoying each other's company. The property's character showed in details like the dual wagon wheels lining the driveway entrance and Grandma's beautiful garden where she grew collard greens, green beans, and other vegetables. The detached garage housed Grandpa's tools along with an old green Chevy pickup truck, which I remember for its distinct gasoline smell and manual stick shift on the steering column.

Thanksgiving brought special traditions, including a parade down the street. Grandma would cook chitlins, which despite their notorious smell, became part of my cherished memories. While the odor drove my siblings and me to escape to the Jackson Mall or play outside, it's now a nostalgic reminder of those days. Another family tradition was visiting the Big Apple Inn on Farish Street for hot tamales: Mom always insisted on getting at least a dozen to take back to Houston.

The neighborhood characters were as memorable as the setting. There was Mr. Washington, distinguished by his salt-and-pepper afro, and Ms. Brown across the street, whom we playfully called a gypsy. She had chickens that she'd command "gone on round that house" as the chickens would go in a choreographed fashion around the house in order to eat their food for the day—something that always made us giggle as children. The area landmarks just off Woodrow Wilson Avenue, a main artery to her neighborhood, included the train tracks, Glorioso's grocery store (now closed), the Jackson Municipal Golf Course, and the Jackson Zoo. Evening porch-sitting meant waving to passing cars as Grandma seemed to know everyone, and neighbors would often stop by to chat.

When I booked our travel on July 15th for this homecoming weekend, I was excited to share these memories with my wife, Kim. We arrived in Jackson just after 10:15 a.m. on Friday, November 1st. Before checking into our hotel, I was determined to revisit Grandma's old home, straight from the airport—a decision that would prove emotionally challenging.

The drive from the airport took about twenty-five minutes, during which I reflected on my deceased loved ones: my mother (passed in 2002), father (2017), and both grandparents. As we turned onto the familiar street from Woodrow Wilson Avenue, my childhood memories collided harshly with present-day reality. What I found was more than simple decay: it was a complete transformation of the community I once knew and loved. The neighborhood had deteriorated dramatically. Approximately 10 percent of the homes stood as badly burned-out charred shells still standing, while another 20 percent were outright abandoned, swallowed by overgrown weeds and trash.

Grandma's house was particularly heartbreaking. The once-proud home that held so many cherished memories had fallen into severe disrepair with its unwelcoming appearance. The house itself showed signs of prolonged neglect, its former warmth and dignity stripped away by years of poor maintenance. The detached garage, though still standing on the property, had completely collapsed. What was once a cared-for garden had become a sad reflection of neglect. Where flowers or vegetables may have once grown, an old toilet now sat among scattered tires and broken debris—the current owner had allowed the home to become a makeshift dumping ground where beauty had been replaced by abandonment.

Across the street, a burned-out house with a blackened frame and broken windows frozen in time stood as a haunting symbol of decline. The few maintained homes seemed like islands in a sea of abandonment, and I could only imagine how their residents felt returning home each day to such dispiriting surroundings. The once-inviting front porches where neighbors would gather now faced scenes of urban decay rather than the friendly passing cars of my childhood.

The scene across the street only amplified the devastation. Where I remembered a neighbor's well-kept home now stood a scorched, empty structure. It appeared the city had simply extinguished the fire and left the structure to rot, suggesting either an inability to locate the property owners or, more likely, that the home had been abandoned long before the fire. This pattern of decay repeated house after house down the street.

I could only manage a single pass down the street before turning around; the contrast between my rich memories and this harsh reality was too stark to bear. It was my first experience of having treasured memories so completely contradicted by present-day reality, and the emotional impact left me quiet and contemplative as we drove away. The neighborhood that had once exemplified the strength of a close-knit Black community now stood as a stark reminder of economic abandonment.

Jackson's abandoned property crisis—accounting for nearly 25 percent of all such properties in Mississippi—is the result of a deeply rooted and interconnected set of challenges. Mississippi ranks among the states with the highest poverty rates in the country, and Jackson contributes significantly to that statistic. The city's struggles stem from a long history of racial inequality and systemic discrimination, compounded by economic hardships, lack of corporate investment, and underfunded infrastructure. These conditions have led to fewer quality jobs, educational disparities, and a persistent sense of inadequate support from the state government. As residents leave in search of better opportunities, population decline follows—dragging down property values and tax revenues. All of these factors contribute to the growing issue of property tax delinquency and widespread abandonment across Jackson.

Downtown Jackson, where we checked into our hotel, felt frozen in time rather than modern and vibrant. Red brick buildings and poorly maintained streets spoke of a city struggling to keep pace with contemporary development. While we felt safe at the hotel, the city's atmosphere lacked the energy and optimism found in more prosperous urban centers.

Around lunchtime, I was eager to revisit the Big Apple Inn on Farish Street. The small establishment remained authentically unchanged, with its charmingly simple menu: tamales for takeout, and $2.10 sandwiches: choices of smoked sausage, pig ear, hamburger, hot dog, or bologna. Cheese was an extra 25 cents, chips 55 cents, and drinks came from a vending machine. The nostalgic touches remained: an old fortune-telling body weight scale and a *Jackson Advocate* newspaper dispenser stood as witnesses to bygone times.

The ordering process was old-school: the cashier wrote orders on repurposed cardboard from soda boxes. When my wife asked about "what comes on the hamburger?", the cashier's response of "evathang" spoke volumes about the no-frills approach. We ordered a few smoked sausage sandwiches and a couple of hamburgers, and we were soon joined by Mitch and his wife Dede, first-time visitors to this establishment. They added pig ear sandwiches to our feast, and we were later joined by one of Mitch's classmates, turning lunch into an hour-long social gathering. I made sure to order six hot tamales; they were as delicious as I remembered.

By 2:15 p.m., we headed to Jackson State University for the traditional hanging out on the yard: a cornerstone of homecoming festivities. The campus was alive with current students, alumni reunions, and members of the Divine Nine—a collaborative council of nine historically Black fraternities and sororities—all socializing and enjoying music and food under the cloudy, warm sky. Everyone was having a great time. Mitch and his wife reconnected with old friends while giving us a campus tour, pointing out significant buildings, and sharing university history. We captured countless photos before heading to the Iron Horse Grill for dinner with our growing group, now eight strong.

Saturday morning began early, with Kim and I having breakfast at the hotel around 8 a.m. Though kickoff wasn't until 2:30 p.m., we knew tailgating would be an all-day affair. I dressed in my Jackson State Tigers hat I had bought online and navy blue T-shirt, while Kim, a proud member of Delta Sigma Theta, wore her sorority shirt with casual pants and matching Jordans. After recording my customary game day video around 10 a.m., we met Mitch and Dede in the lobby to head out together to the stadium.

We arrived at Mississippi Veterans Memorial Stadium just before 10:30 in the morning, and the sight that greeted us was nothing short of spectacular. RVs stretched across the parking lot as far as the eye could see—not just any RVs, but predominantly massive, bus-sized luxury vehicles, each staking its claim to a piece of the homecoming celebration. The air was already electric with anticipation and festivity.

The parking lot had transformed into a sprawling city of tailgaters, with pickup trucks interspersed among the RVs, each setup more elaborate than the last. Custom tents dotted the landscape, their blue and white colors paying homage to Jackson State, while the rhythmic blend of multiple sound systems created a soundtrack for the day. The sweet, smoky aroma of dozens of barbecue smokers filled the air, each contributing its own signature to the symphony of scents.

Mitch's family had secured prime real estate, setting up a few tents that served as their homecoming headquarters. Their setup was impressive—a DJ had already started creating his own pocket of energy in the vast celebration. The food spread was nothing short of magnificent, with ribs slowly smoking, sausages sizzling, hamburgers grilling, and chicken cooking to perfection. Drinks were flowing from non-alcoholic to a variety of adult spirits as well. This wasn't just a tailgate; it was a full-scale family reunion combined with a Southern culinary showcase.

The 61,000-seat stadium loomed above the festivities, its concrete facade serving as a backdrop to the unfolding celebration. While the venue itself stood slightly removed from Jackson State's campus, this separation seemed irrelevant as the parking lot had been transformed into an extension of the university's culture and spirit. The Tiger faithful had claimed it as their own for this homecoming celebration, with an expected crowd of 35,000 set to fill its seats later that day.

The energy was infectious, with early arrivers already setting up elaborate food stations, testing sound systems, and establishing their territories for what promised to be an epic day of celebration. This wasn't just pregame preparation: it was the beginning of a day-long festival where the actual football game would be just one part of a much larger celebration of HBCU culture and community.

Mitch and I set out to explore the full scope of this homecoming tailgate experience. The "Sip & Chill Mobile Bar," run by "Steve the Bartender," was our first discovery—an entrepreneurial setup that rivaled any professional mobile bar I'd seen. Steve's specialty was his hand grenades, frozen concoctions that packed both flavor and punch. Mitch and I each ordered two, and Steve's expertise was evident in every sip.

The true essence of Southern tailgating culture revealed itself as I ventured deeper into the crowd. I first encountered Demetrius, who had a smoker that was releasing the most intoxicating aroma of post oak wood mixed with slow-cooked ribs and brisket. When I explained my fourteen-week bucket list journey, he insisted I sample his handiwork. The brisket was absolutely delicious—perfectly seasoned with a smoke ring that spoke of hours of patient cooking.

Not far away, Jeffrey's setup stopped me in my tracks. He'd brought what could only be described as a professional-grade operation: a massive fifteen-foot-long smoker that was handling multiple meats simultaneously. Ribs, sausage, and brisket slowly cooked while releasing heavenly aromas. But Jeffrey hadn't stopped at just food; he'd established a full-service bar offering both alcoholic and non-alcoholic beverages. His sausage, which he generously shared, had the perfect snap and seasoning that only comes from years of perfecting a recipe.

But it was Julius who took tailgating to an entirely different level. This brother had brought an entire hibachi station to the parking lot, and he was working it like a master chef. The spread was mind-boggling: succulent shrimp sizzling on the flat top, chicken being expertly flipped, lamb chops cooking to perfection, ribs glazing beautifully, and steak hitting just the right temperature. As if that wasn't enough, he had fried chicken on a stick, fresh fish, crispy french fries, and delectable baked beans.

Julius's bar setup was equally impressive as every type of spirit was represented: premium vodkas, top-shelf tequilas, an array of dark liquors, and every mixer imaginable. Julius took special care of me, insisting I sample his creations.

Each of these encounters represented Southern hospitality and HBCU tailgating culture. Everyone I met welcomed me warmly, eager to share their food, drinks, and stories. The fact that I was experiencing their homecoming celebration for my bucket list journey seemed to make them even more determined to ensure I got the full experience.

By 1:00 p.m., the atmosphere was electric. Line dancing broke out at Mitch's tailgate spot as the DJ kept the energy high playing "Fall-N" by Chingy. We made our way to the stadium shortly afterward, where Kim and I took photos with each other along with the JSU field logo as a backdrop. Thanks to fellow J-State alum Len and his wife Thais, we secured perfect seats near the end zone, where Len shared insider knowledge about Jackson State traditions.

A distinct rumble of drums began to build from the far side of the stadium. Len said, "Watch this—you're about to see something special." The Sonic Boom of the South, Jackson State's renowned marching band, was making their entrance, and even before they came into view, their presence was announced by the thunderous percussion section.

As they rounded the corner into view, it was a spectacular display of precision and showmanship. The band members marched in perfect formation, their blue and white uniforms crisp and gleaming in the afternoon sun. Len directed my attention to a unique JSU tradition: the freshman band members marching with their bottom lips protruding, a subtle identifier of their first-year status that brought knowing smiles from alumni in the crowd.

While the full band was moving in perfect synchronization, it was primarily the drum section providing the soundtrack for their entrance. The rhythmic cadence echoed through the stadium, each beat seeming to pulse through the crowd. Other band members maintained their formation with military precision, instruments ready but not yet playing, creating a powerful visual of disciplined anticipation.

The spectacle wasn't limited to just the band. The auxiliary units, including the dancers known as the Prancing J-Settes, moved with incredible grace and energy, adding their own flair to the entrance. As they passed our section, you could feel the energy surge through the crowd. Alumni stood, many swaying to the drum cadence, while others recorded the moment on their phones, knowing they were witnessing a signature element of HBCU culture.

The band settled into their designated section, just two sections over from where we sat, perfectly positioning us to experience their full impact throughout the game.

The placement proved perfect for what was to come—close enough that we could distinguish individual instruments and see the expressions of determination and pride on the musicians' faces as they prepared to provide the soundtrack for this homecoming celebration. This entrance was more than just a band taking their seats; it was the opening ceremony of what would prove to be an unforgettable display of HBCU culture and tradition.

The actual football game kicked off at 2 p.m., with Jackson State immediately asserting their dominance over Arkansas Pine Bluff. But what made this game uniquely special wasn't just the action on the field—it was the constant musical backdrop provided by both bands. Unlike traditional college football where bands typically play only during specific breaks, the HBCU experience featured an ongoing musical conversation between the two schools' bands. During every timeout, defensive stand, or momentary lull in play, either JSU's Sonic Boom of the South or Arkansas Pine Bluff's band would burst into contemporary R&B hits, keeping the crowd energized and on their feet.

Jackson State's football team put on an offensive clinic, building a commanding 31–3 lead by halftime. But everyone knew the real show was about to begin. As the teams headed to their locker rooms, there was a shift in energy throughout the stadium. The halftime show at an HBCU game isn't just an intermission: it's often considered the main event, and today would prove why.

The University of Arkansas Pine Bluff's Marching Musical Machine of the Mid-South (M4) took the field first. Their performance was impressive, featuring the Dazz Band's "Let It Whip" among other selections. Their precision drilling, synchronized movements, and musical prowess set a high bar for what was to come. The dance crew (Golden Girls) and cheerleaders added their own dynamic elements, creating a complete performance that had the crowd fully engaged.

Then came the moment everyone had been waiting for: the Sonic Boom of the South's homecoming performance. Jackson State's band had crafted a spectacular tribute to Michael Jackson, and from the first note, it was clear this would be something special. They opened with a soul-stirring rendition of The Jackson Five tune "I'll Be There," the formation and sound so perfect it sent chills through the stadium.

The energy escalated as they transitioned into "Beat It," with the band members executing intricate formations while maintaining impeccable sound quality. The drum majors took center stage during "Bad," showcasing their remarkable showmanship with high-stepping moves and dramatic flourishes that Michael himself might have appreciated.

But it was their finale, "Thriller," that brought the house down. The entire band moved in perfect synchronization, re-creating iconic Michael Jackson dance moves while playing with flawless precision. The drum line's cadence matched the familiar beat perfectly, while the brass section delivered those signature "Thriller" notes with power and clarity. The J-Settes added their own spectacular choreography, their movements synchronized perfectly with the music.

The performance wasn't just about playing songs: it was a complete visual and musical experience. The band moved through complex formations, creating visual representations of Michael Jackson's signature moves and symbols on the field while maintaining exceptional sound quality. The precision of their movements, the power of their music, and the creativity of their show design demonstrated why HBCU bands are considered among the best in the nation.

The crowd remained standing throughout the entire halftime show, many dancing and singing along, others recording on their phones, knowing they were witnessing something special. When the final notes of "Thriller" echoed through the stadium, the roar from the crowd was deafening—a recognition that they had just witnessed not just a halftime show, but a masterpiece of musicianship, choreography, and showmanship that embodied the very best of HBCU culture and tradition.

The first half and halftime show had set a high bar for the rest of the afternoon, proving that HBCU football games offer an entertainment experience that goes far beyond just the action on the field. It was a celebration of music, culture, and excellence that would continue well into the second half.

The football game itself ended decisively, with Jackson State delivering a commanding 41–3 victory over Arkansas Pine Bluff. Yet unlike traditional college games where fans rush to beat the traffic, the stadium remained packed. Veterans of HBCU football games knew that one of the day's most anticipated traditions was about to unfold: the "Fifth Quarter."

As the players cleared the field, both bands settled into position for what would be a thirty-minute musical showdown. This wasn't a mere postgame performance but a serious battle of the bands: Arkansas Pine Bluff's M4 versus Jackson State's Sonic Boom of the South. The unwritten rules were straightforward. Each band would have approximately two minutes per round to showcase their talents, trading performances back and forth in an attempt to outshine their opponent. With bands seated on opposing sides of the stands, this created its own field of play.

Pine Bluff opened the battle with a dynamic arrangement of Beyoncé's "Naughty Girl," their horns crisp and clear while the Golden Girls executed perfectly synchronized moves. Jackson State countered powerfully with the Gap Band's "My Heart Is Yearning for Your Love," their brass section demonstrating why they're called the Sonic Boom of the South. The musical volleyball continued as Pine Bluff delivered Whitney Houston's "I Have Nothing," showcasing their range and versatility. Jackson State responded with Tony Terry's "With You," their arrangement drawing massive cheers from the crowd.

Each band incorporated their full arsenal: drum majors leading with spectacular high-stepping routines, dancing girls executing intricate choreography, and musicians displaying their mastery through both classic and contemporary selections. The percussion sections were particularly impressive, their cadences driving each performance with precision and power.

What made the Fifth Quarter special wasn't just the music: it was the total package of entertainment. Everything from the selection of songs to the timing of dance moves was choreographed to perfection. The bands incorporated "hype songs" that got the remaining crowd of nearly thirty-five thousand on their feet, turning the stadium into what felt like an outdoor concert.

The bands played back and forth, neither willing to concede an inch in this friendly but fierce competition. They pulled out all stops—popular hip-hop hits, R&B classics, and even some original arrangements that showcased their musical creativity. Each band's dancing squads— Pine Bluff's Golden Girls and Jackson State's Prancing J-Settes—added their own flair to the performances, executing routines that looked more like professional dance numbers than typical marching band accompaniment.

The Fifth Quarter concluded around 5:45 p.m., having delivered a spectacular display of HBCU band culture that rivaled, if not surpassed, the excitement of the football game itself. While Jackson State may have dominated on the field, both bands proved themselves champions during this extraordinary musical battle.

The crowd finally began dispersing close to 6 p.m., but not to head home. Instead, most people simply transferred the celebration back to the parking lot, where the tailgating would continue well into the evening. The Fifth Quarter had provided the perfect bridge between the official game and the extended homecoming festivities that would follow, exemplifying the unique blend of sport, music, and culture that makes HBCU football games such remarkable events.

By 6 p.m., the parking lot had transformed into an even more vibrant celebration than the pregame festivities. Kim and I, along with Mitch, Dede, Len, and Thais, made our way back to our tailgate spot, where the party was reaching new heights. The setting sun did nothing to diminish the energy: if anything, it seemed to intensify the celebration.

The atmosphere had shifted from gameday revelry to full-on homecoming festival. The music pumping through various speakers seemed louder. The food was still flowing—grills reignited for evening cooking sessions, and coolers opened back up for postgame refreshments. The earlier atmosphere of casual sampling had evolved into full-on evening dining, with people gathering in groups to share meals and stories. The smell of barbecue still permeated the air, mixing with the sound of laughter and music to create a multi-sensory celebration.

The parking lot had become a sprawling block party. Some RVs had deployed their exterior televisions, creating gathering spots for people to watch other college football games. The professional-level sound systems that some tailgaters had brought were now being used to their full potential. The variety of music created different zones of celebration throughout the lot.

Individuals and organizations took center stage when songs like "Flex" by The Party Boyz came on, with fraternities and sororities showcasing their signature steps, strolls, and calls. The precision and energy of their line dances drew circles of spectators, with members from different chapters joining in as the display of Greek unity and tradition added another dimension to the already rich cultural celebration.

Though the festivities showed no signs of slowing down and would likely continue well into the night, Kim and I along with Mitch and Dede decided to wind down our day around 8 p.m. We had been on the grounds since morning, experiencing every aspect of this remarkable HBCU homecoming tradition. Before leaving, Kim and I recorded our final video of the day, capturing the still-energetic atmosphere and reflecting on the full experience of Jackson State's homecoming celebration.

The postgame tailgate served as a perfect conclusion to our day, demonstrating that HBCU homecoming isn't just about football or even about the gameday experience: it's about community, culture, and celebration in its purest form. As we left the grounds, the music, laughter, and festivities continued behind us, the parking lot still pulsing with the energy of thousands celebrating this cherished tradition.

Week Ten of my journey stirred complex emotions: from the sobering reality of Grandma's neighborhood to the jubilant celebration of black college culture. As we recorded our final video of the day, I was already looking forward to Week Eleven's matchup between Florida A&M and Prairie View A&M back in Texas. The day had perfectly encapsulated both the challenges facing many historic black communities and the enduring spirit that continues to bring people together in celebration of their shared culture and traditions.

FLORIDA A&M AT PRAIRIE VIEW A&M

As Week Eleven approached in early August, I had initially considered several attractive matchups including Alabama at LSU, Mississippi State at Tennessee, Washington at Penn State, and New Mexico at San Diego State. While some of these venues were appealing, I was trying to avoid locations I'd previously visited, even though games like the LSU-Alabama contest would have been worth considering for an exceptional matchup.

My plans took an unexpected turn when I learned about a friend's birthday celebration in Mexico during that week. Initially, I thought Week Eleven would become a skip in my bucket list journey, assuming the travel logistics would be too complicated. However, fate had other plans.

In October, I revisited the Week Eleven schedule and discovered an HBCU game in Texas: Florida A&M Rattlers versus Prairie View Panthers. This brought to mind a conversation with my friend Steve, whom I'd seen the previous year in Austin. He had mentioned having season tickets to Prairie View games, as his son attended the university. After reaching out to Steve, he enthusiastically invited me to join him, making it possible to maintain my streak of games that kept me close to home.

On the morning of November 9th, I woke up at 8 a.m. and dressed in a purple polo shirt. Just before 9 a.m., I recorded my customary weekly gameday video in my driveway. With the game scheduled for 2 p.m., I arrived at Prairie View shortly after 11 a.m. following a quick drive up Highway 290.

Prairie View A&M University, located fifty miles northwest of Houston, is an intimate campus of about 10,000 students with a stadium capacity of 15,000. After parking on campus shortly after 11 a.m., I set out to explore Prairie View A&M on foot. The walk to the stadium was about a quarter mile, but I took my time exploring the grounds. The campus was notably quiet that morning, with few students about, making it easy to find parking and explore at my leisure.

My wandering first led me to a remarkable discovery: the William H. Holland and Matthew Gaines Memorial Park. I paused here, taking time to read and reflect upon the memorial plaque. Both Holland and Gaines emerged as fascinating historical figures who had played pivotal roles in shaping Prairie View A&M through their contributions to both education and politics. The park served as a fitting tribute to their legacy.

Continuing my exploration through the beautifully maintained campus, I could easily understand its appeal to mostly area students. The proximity to Houston combined with the serene, academic atmosphere created an ideal environment for learning. My path took me to the Tempton Memorial Student Center, where I purchased a purple Prairie View hat to show my support for the day's game. The student center housed not only the bookstore but other typical campus union facilities such as dining options and administrative facilities.

From there, I continued exploring down Minor Street, following it until I reached Preston Street. The campus architecture and landscaping were particularly impressive, with well-maintained buildings and manicured grounds creating an inviting collegiate atmosphere. The intimate scale of the ten-thousand-student campus gave it a welcoming feel, neither too vast nor too compact.

My campus tour ultimately led me to the Blackshear Stadium parking lot, where the early signs of tailgating were beginning to appear. This transition from the academic heart of campus to the gameday festivities provided a perfect glimpse into both the educational and social aspects of Prairie View A&M's campus life.

As noon approached, the Blackshear Stadium parking lot was coming alive with tailgate preparations. I made my way over to what turned out to be the alumni tent, where I met Dennis, a proud Prairie View graduate who immediately embraced me as if I were a longtime friend. When I shared my story about the fourteen-week bucket list journey, he reacted with, "now that's what I'm talking about, that's living it up."

The alumni tailgate setup was impressive, featuring a spread of food catered by BEAUX, one of the male campus organizations. The atmosphere was enhanced by music from a DJ and the growing excitement of arriving fans. Dennis and I spent considerable time talking about his experiences at Prairie View and his daughter, who had followed in his footsteps by attending the university. Dennis spoke highly of Prairie View and credited his career advancements to both his experiences there and the networking opportunities that followed. He made sure to introduce me to several other alumni, each eager to share their own Prairie View stories—tales of lifelong friendships formed in the dorms, unforgettable homecomings, favorite professors who left lasting impressions, and the challenges that shaped who they are today. It quickly became clear that their connection to Prairie View ran deep, rooted in pride and shaped by a shared sense of purpose and belonging.

While the parking lot wasn't yet at full capacity, several alumni assured me that even though this wasn't homecoming weekend, I was in for a treat. The conversation frequently turned to homecoming, with Dennis particularly insistent that I should return the following year for that experience. When I mentioned I'd just attended Jackson State's homecoming the previous week, this sparked some friendly competitive banter as he mentioned, "J-State can't compete with us. I've been to other HBCU homecomings and I'll tell ya, our week long celebration tops 'em all – the tailgates, the food, the giveback events put us at the top."

I then made my way to the Day One Crew PVU tent, where I met Ken and enjoyed sharing my bucket list story with him as well. The tailgating scene continued to grow more elaborate, with RVs of various sizes rolling in, from modest setups to impressive bus-sized vehicles. Every group I encountered showed the same welcoming spirit, each emphasizing that while today would be fun, I really needed to experience a Prairie View homecoming to see tailgating at its finest. When I mentioned my recent Jackson State experience, it drew good-natured laughter from the alumni, who were confident their homecoming could match any other HBCU celebration. This vibrant tailgating scene set the perfect tone for what would prove to be a memorable afternoon of HBCU football culture.

At one o'clock, the energy in the parking lot shifted as the Prairie

View band, Marching Storm, gathered at the far end, with their drum major leading them through some pregame practice routines. The sound of their rehearsal added another layer of excitement to the already festive atmosphere.

Shortly after the band began practicing, my friend Steve and his wife Lesia arrived. Our reunion was marked with warm hugs and embraces, and they suggested we head back to the alumni tent for lunch before the game. We made our way over, where Steve and Lesia reconnected with fellow alumni they hadn't seen in a while. I enjoyed listening to them catch up and share family updates, the conversation flowing easily among old friends.

With kickoff scheduled for 2 p.m., we decided to make our way to the stadium around 1:45. Despite being early November, the Texas heat was still in full force, with temperatures pushing into the upper 80s, possibly even touching the low 90s. The stadium entrance impressed me: this was clearly a modern facility, featuring a well-designed two-tier setup that had been built relatively recently.

Though I had general admission tickets, Steve and Lesia graciously invited me to sit with them in their seats on the twenty-yard line, about ten rows up. Our location provided an unobstructed view of the field and positioned us perfectly to watch the Marching Storm. As we approached the two o'clock kickoff, the stadium was about half full, and the Prairie View band elevated the energy by performing Juvenile's "Back That Azz Up," setting the tone for what would be an entertaining afternoon of football. From our vantage point, we had a perfect view of the pregame festivities, watching the cheerleaders enter with their Prairie A&M flags while the band and dancers performed, creating the perfect HBCU gameday atmosphere as the team made their entrance onto the field.

Steve and I settled into our seats for what initially appeared to be heading toward a lopsided affair. Despite Florida A&M's reputation for having a solid team this season, Prairie View quickly established dominance on the field. As the game unfolded, Steve and I found ourselves entertained not just by the action on the field, but by the passionate fans around us. We shared several laughs watching some particularly animated supporters who were intensely invested in every play, constantly shouting for the Prairie View team to perform better, even as they maintained a comfortable lead. One woman in particular stood out—she was decked out head to toe in purple and gold, from her glittery sneakers to her custom Panther earrings, and she wasn't shy about letting the team hear her expectations. Passionately clapping her hands with every down, she shouted with full voice, "Let's go, let's go, give me a tackle, I wanna see a tackle, play like you know whatchu doing, let's go, tackle!" It was clear she didn't just attend the games—she lived them. By halftime, Prairie View had built a commanding 17–3 advantage.

Then came the highlight of the day: the Prairie View A&M Marching Storm's halftime performance. Their show was nothing short of spectacular, demonstrating why they're considered one of the premier HBCU bands in the country. In a particularly memorable moment, they performed an innovative arrangement of the *Entertainment Tonight* theme song that had the crowd on their feet. I never imagined this familiar TV theme tune could be transformed into such a dynamic, energetic performance, but the Marching Storm managed to do just that with impressive style.

The band continued to electrify the crowd with their rendition of Ludacris's "Act a Fool," seamlessly blending other selections into their performance that kept the energy at peak levels throughout the entire halftime show. The combination of the precision drumline, powerful horn section, and the dynamic dancers created an unforgettable spectacle. As I watched, I couldn't help but think about what their homecoming performance must be like, given that everyone had told me these shows were even more spectacular. The halftime show alone made me seriously consider returning the following year for homecoming, just to witness what the Marching Storm would do with an even bigger stage.

The second half of the game followed a similar pattern to the first, with Florida A&M's offense continuing to struggle. Their difficulties were compounded by several costly turnovers, including a couple of interceptions and a fumble. Prairie View capitalized on these mistakes, ultimately securing a convincing 31–12 victory. As the game wound down around five o'clock, we were treated to a beautiful Texas sunset, and despite the one-sided score, the Prairie View faithful maintained their enthusiasm until the final whistle.

The game officially concluded just after 5:15 p.m., and I took a moment to record my closing video for the week. I reflected on the day's highlights: the welcoming atmosphere at the tailgate festivities, the precious time spent with my good friend Steve and his wife, and the incredible performance by the Prairie View A&M Marching Storm. The combination of good football, great music, and warm hospitality had made for another memorable entry in my bucket list journey.

After wrapping up the video, Steve, Lesia, and I made our way back to the tailgate area, but found that most folks had already started packing up and heading home. As I said my goodbyes and began my two-hour drive home, my mind was already drifting to the following week's adventure: a trip to Atlanta with Kim. I'd make my way to Athens on Saturday to watch Tennessee take on Georgia—a highly anticipated SEC showdown—but just as exciting was the chance for us to spend quality time with family while we were in town. It was shaping up to be another weekend of football, food, and familiar faces. The relatively short journey home was a welcome change from some of my longer football trips, giving me time to appreciate how this surprise addition to my schedule had turned into such a wonderful experience.

While I hadn't initially planned to include Prairie View A&M in my bucket list tour, it had proven to be a fortunate addition. The day had offered everything that makes college football special: passionate fans, good food, exciting football, outstanding band performances, and the unique culture of HBCU gameday traditions. As I drove home under the Texas stars, I found myself seriously considering everyone's suggestion to return for next year's homecoming.

#7 TENNESSEE AT #12 GEORGIA

Week Twelve's destination was decided on my birthday, August 14th, as I sorted through several attractive matchups. Having already visited some venues and seen certain teams play, I was able to narrow down my choices. Missouri vs. South Carolina was out since I'd seen South Carolina in Week Three, and Virginia at Notre Dame was eliminated as I'd already experienced Notre Dame in Week One (plus the potential for chilly weather was a deterrent in South Bend). Utah at Colorado was also off the list since I'd been to Colorado in Week Five.

Two games emerged as strong contenders: LSU at Florida and Tennessee at Georgia. The Georgia game particularly intrigued me for several reasons. I'd always wanted to see the famous hedges at Sanford Stadium: those distinctive bushes lining the field and endzone that I'd seen on TV since childhood. Additionally, Athens' proximity to Atlanta meant my wife could join me on the trip and visit her family while I attended the game. Though there was another Georgia game in Week Fourteen, it fell on the Friday after Thanksgiving, when Atlanta travel could be challenging. The decision was made: we were heading to Atlanta for Tennessee vs. Georgia.

My wife and I flew to Atlanta on Thursday, November 14th, staying with her cousin Anasa. Thursday was spent catching up, and Friday brought an unexpected treat as we attended a surprise birthday party for Anasa's mother Patt. The timing worked perfectly; while I would head to Athens for Saturday's game, my wife and her family had planned a spa day and fish fry.

I'd prepared for gameday by purchasing a University of Georgia hat to wear with my red t-shirt, blue jeans, and tennis shoes, plus a jacket in case temperatures dropped. This was shaping up to be a crucial matchup: a 7:30 p.m. primetime kickoff between #12 Georgia and #7 Tennessee, with ESPN's College GameDay in attendance. Remarkably, this would be the sixth game I attended this season for which GameDay was on site for their telecast (did I mention ESPN was following me around?).

Saturday morning began around 7:30, following my usual gameday routine. After breakfast and getting dressed, I hit the road by 8:30 for the two-hour drive to Athens. Though I hoped to catch some of College GameDay, I wasn't going to rush: if I made it in time, great; if not, there would be plenty else to see. Before departing, I recorded my traditional pregame video under perfect football conditions: mid-50s temperature, forecast to reach the mid-70s, with clear blue skies.

The drive to Athens was smooth and straightforward, with minimal traffic given the nine-hour cushion before kickoff. I entered Sanford Stadium into my GPS mainly to get my bearings on campus, knowing that public parking near the stadium would likely be restricted to season ticket holders. As I approached, some streets were still open, but rather than waste time searching for non-existent stadium parking, I did some quick research. I discovered that College GameDay was broadcasting from Myers Quad, so I focused my parking search in that area. Fortune smiled on me as I found neighborhood street parking about a half-mile from the Quad around 10:45 a.m. After a short walk up DW Brooks Drive, I passed a few early tailgaters in the engineering and veterinary school lots en route to campus.

By 11:00 a.m., I had made it to the GameDay setup, with about an hour remaining in the broadcast. The scene was familiar from my previous GameDay experiences: multiple TV screens, creative fan-made signs, and the iconic "Ol Crimson" flag that appears at every broadcast. I managed to get photos with Hairy Dawg, Georgia's mascot, as well as various inflatable Bulldog mascots around the set. The atmosphere crackled with electricity, dominated by Georgia fans but with a solid contingent of Tennessee supporters mixed in.

Around 11:05 a.m., I witnessed the traditional Pat McAfee's field goal challenge, where a selected student had a chance to win over $200,000 by successfully kicking a thirty-three yard field goal. The pressure proved too much, and the kick was missed:—a reminder of how challenging it must be to perform under that kind of pressure with so many eyes watching.

At 11:30 a.m., the Myers Quad was beginning its transformation. While College GameDay was winding down, tailgating tents started popping up across the landscape. The aroma of barbecue smoke began wafting through the air, and I decided to follow my instincts (and my nose) to the very first tent I encountered. There I met Sims, and what began as a casual introduction turned into one of the day's most memorable connections.

I shared my bucket list journey with him, and his eyes lit up with immediate interest. As we talked, we discovered a coincidental connection: Sims had actually been in Austin for Week Eight when Georgia played Texas. This shared experience opened up an animated conversation about football, travel, and traditions. Sims, I learned, wasn't just a casual fan but a dedicated Georgia alum who took his tailgating seriously.

He detailed his upcoming spread for the day: they would be grilling burgers and hot dogs, smoking ribs, preparing grilled chicken, and serving a special shrimp casserole, along with both alcoholic and non-alcoholic beverages. This wasn't just a casual setup; Sims explained that his tailgate typically hosted between thirty to forty people for every home game. As a devoted alumnus, he made it a point to travel to one or two road games each season to support his Bulldogs.

Despite the fact that his tailgate wasn't fully set up yet—the main festivities would begin in the early to mid-afternoon—Sims extended a warm invitation for me to return later. His hospitality was genuine and enthusiastic, a perfect example of the Southern football hospitality I'd encountered throughout my journey. This first interaction set a promising tone for what would prove to be an exceptional game day in Athens.

Moving on from Sims's tent, I found myself at the next setup where I met John, who was tending to his smoker with focused attention. The rich aroma of slow-cooked meat drew me in, and he greeted me with an enthusiastic "Go Dawgs!" before introducing me to what he called his "beef on wick"—his special take on pulled pork sandwiches. Despite the name suggesting beef, his pork creation was a testament to his smoking expertise. When I mentioned it was my first time in Athens, John immediately offered me a sample, and the flavors lived up to the enticing smell. This early taste test suggested I was in for a memorable day of tailgating cuisine.

As noon approached, the crowd began gravitating back toward the College GameDay set for the highly anticipated picks segment. The energy around the set was electric as the analysts made their predictions for the evening's clash between #12 Georgia and #7 Tennessee. The crowd erupted with cheers as each analyst sided with Georgia, only to switch to playful boos when Desmond Howard broke ranks and picked Tennessee to pull off the upset.

The segment built to its traditional crescendo: Lee Corso's headgear pick. The moment became even more special when Uga, Georgia's beloved live mascot, was brought onto the set. In classic Corso fashion, he played to the crowd before donning the Georgia Bulldog mascot head, sending the assembled fans into a frenzy. The interaction between Corso and Uga, as the two mascots (one live, one human) shared the stage, created the kind of magical moment that makes College GameDay a special part of college football tradition. The synchronicity of Corso's theatrics, Uga's presence, and the crowd's reaction perfectly captured the pageantry of college football, providing a fitting end to the morning's festivities.

After College GameDay concluded, I spent time introducing myself to various fans around the Quad, consistently meeting with enthusiasm when sharing my bucket list journey. These conversations had become a familiar and enjoyable part of my weekly adventures, with people asking similar questions about my motivation, the games I'd attended, cost of the journey, and the logistics of planning such an ambitious schedule. The interest and excitement from fellow college football enthusiasts never got old.

Seeking a brief respite from the growing crowds and wanting to explore more of campus, I made my way to the Tate Student Center. This proved to be a perfect mid-day decision, as I ended up spending a couple of hours there. The facility was impressive, offering a comprehensive hub of student life. With YouTube TV available on my phone and comfortable seating areas throughout, I found an ideal spot to rest and recharge, knowing the day ahead would be long.

The Tate Student Center was a microcosm of university life, featuring an array of dining options for students, administrative offices handling various student affairs, and practical amenities including a game room and printing services. Its strategic location near the stadium made it a natural gathering point, and I enjoyed watching the steady stream of students, parents, and fans flowing through the building.

The large seating area provided an excellent vantage point for people-watching, as the center grew increasingly busy with gameday visitors. The mix of everyday student life and gameday excitement created an interesting dynamic, with the building serving both its regular university function and as a comfortable refuge for visitors like myself seeking a break from the outdoor festivities.

During my time there, I used the opportunity to rest my feet, catch some of the early games on my phone, and observe the gradual transformation of campus as more and more fans arrived for the evening's big game. The comfortable, air-conditioned environment offered a perfect contrast to the growing energy outside, allowing me to pace myself for the long day ahead. This blend of relaxation and observation time proved to be a smart strategic decision in managing my energy for the primetime kickoff still hours away.

The Tate Student Center's atmosphere perfectly embodied what I'd come to love about college football: the way these games become central to campus life while remaining just one part of the broader university experience. It provided a welcome glimpse into daily life at Georgia beyond the pageantry of game day, adding another layer to my understanding of the institution I was visiting.

Around 2 p.m., I decided to follow up on a meaningful connection from Week Eight: Roger, whom I'd met during the Texas vs. Georgia game in Austin. He had extended an invitation to visit his tailgate at the Legion parking lot if I made it to Athens. Without his phone number but armed with the memory of our selfie together (and his distinctive appearance), I walked through the lot, introducing myself to various groups until I spotted him.

Roger, distinguished by his gray hair and beard, was decked out in Georgia gear. When our eyes met, his expression shifted from initial confusion to delighted recognition. What could have been an awkward moment transformed into a warm reunion, as if we were old friends reconnecting. The sincere pleasure in his welcome validated one of the best aspects of my journey: the authentic connections formed through college football. We recorded another video together to document our reunion, and though his tailgate setup wasn't yet complete, he enthusiastically invited me to return later in the day.

Following this heartwarming reconnection, I continued my exploration of Georgia's campus, making my way along Cloverhurst Avenue. The walk took me past several dining halls, offering a glimpse into everyday student life. Moving along Hall Street, I observed the architectural evolution of campus through its dormitories. The older residence halls—Amos Hall, Benson Hall, and Core Hall—showcased classic red brick construction, standing as testimonies to the university's history.

My path led me northward toward Broad Street, where the campus architecture took on a more imposing character. Here, the administrative buildings and law school facilities projected academic dignity, their design and scale reflecting their institutional importance. The contrast between these different areas of campus told the story of the university's growth and development over time.

This comprehensive campus walk provided a deeper appreciation for the University of Georgia beyond its gameday persona. The blend of historic and modern buildings, academic and residential spaces, created a rich tapestry that helped me understand why this institution held such a special place in its community. As I walked, the growing gameday crowds began interweaving with this architectural backdrop, gradually transforming the academic spaces into a festival of college football enthusiasm.

The intimate scale of some areas—like tucked-away courtyards, or small clusters of students and alumni catching up on folding chairs—contrasted wonderfully with the grandeur of others, such as the expansive Quad filled with fans. Watching this academic institution transform into a gameday destination added another layer to my appreciation of college football culture. Each portion of campus seemed to tell its own story while contributing to the larger narrative of both the university's academic mission and its celebrated football tradition.

By 3 p.m., with kickoff drawing closer and campus swelling with fans and gameday traffic, I made my way back to Sims's tailgate. After wondering around for a bit, I arrived around 3:30 p.m. to find his setup in full swing. The transformation from our morning meeting was impressive: now the area buzzed with energy, laughter, and the irresistible aroma of multiple grills at work.

Sims's tailgate had evolved into exactly what he'd promised and more. The grilled chicken was perfectly done, and the ribs were masterfully prepared, bearing the mark of someone who had perfected their technique over many gamedays. The spread was complemented by flowing drinks and the warm welcome of Sims's fraternity brothers, who embraced me as if I were a longtime member of their gameday family.

Among these new acquaintances, I formed a particularly meaningful connection with Steven, one of Sims's fraternity brothers. Our conversation took an exciting turn when he shared his own upcoming adventure: a planned journey to visit national parks beginning in spring 2025. The synchronicity of meeting another bucket list adventurer was remarkable. We both acknowledged the special nature of this encounter, realizing we were each the first person the other had met who was actively pursuing a bucket list dream. Steven's parting words resonated deeply: "Hey, going across country, you only live once. You better live out your dreams right now."

Sims's tailgate setup exemplified serious dedication to the gameday experience. Comfortable Georgia Bulldogs lawn chairs were arranged for everyone, and a large-screen TV broadcasted the afternoon's college games, creating the perfect atmosphere for football fellowship. His pride and joy was his custom trailer, which he eagerly showed me after a short five-minute walk to the parking lot. The trailer was a testament to his team loyalty, decorated meticulously in Georgia Bulldogs black and red, complemented by Atlanta Falcons logos and proudly displaying a 2022 Bulldogs national championship sticker.

The atmosphere at the tailgate encouraged natural mingling between neighboring setups, creating an inclusive community where fans from various states freely shared stories and experiences. As a Texan, I found myself engaged in fascinating conversations about different football traditions and regional perspectives on the sport. The discussions ranged from comparing barbeque styles to debating conference rivalries, all while watching some play cornhole and enjoy-ing the outstanding food and hospitality.

Around 5:45 p.m., as the anticipation for kickoff began to build, I bid farewell to Sims and his crew. We exchanged contact informa-tion with the intention of staying in touch, whether for future foot-ball gatherings or just to connect if either of us found ourselves in the other's city. The warmth of this tailgate experience perfectly embod-ied the collegiate football spirit: strangers becoming acquaintances through a shared love of the game and the traditions surrounding it.

Making my way to Sanford Stadium required a twenty-minute walk, but anticipation fueled each step. As one of college football's most storied venues, seating 93,000 fans, I was particularly eager to experience what made this stadium special. My ticket placed me in section 211, row 4, seat 22, and I knew I'd be joining the passionate crowd of 42,000 students, devoted alumni, and a strong contingent of visiting Tennessee faithful who had made their presence known throughout the day.

I entered the stadium just before 6 p.m., immediately setting out to see the famous hedges up close. Making my way down as far as possible, I found myself almost giddy with excitement. I captured numerous selfies with the iconic shrubs in the background, and in what might seem like a silly moment to some—but was really cool experience for me—I reached out and actually touched the hedges. For someone who had seen Georgia games on television over the years, always wondering about these distinctive features, it was a bucket list moment within my bucket list journey.

The stadium itself was architecturally impressive, featuring a beau-tiful two-tier design crowned by luxury boxes. As I explored, the dig-ital displays proclaimed "It's Saturday in Athens," providing perfect photo opportunities. The reduced crowd size this early before kickoff allowed me to truly appreciate the venue's design and capture these memorable moments.

With thirty minutes until kickoff, the stadium's digital properties began their choreographed preparation for the game. The Sanford Stadium JumboTron first displayed "Between the Hedges" before transitioning to "It's Time to Tee It Up Between the Hedges," each message drawing growing cheers from the arriving fans. I took advantage of the time to explore both sides of the lower concourse, experiencing perspectives from both the Georgia and Tennessee sections.

The pregame atmosphere intensified with the arrival of Tennessee's band, who did their best to rally their traveling supporters with traditional fight songs like "Rocky Top." However, their efforts were soon overshadowed by Georgia's elaborate pregame festivities. The crowd erupted when Uga, Georgia's beloved live mascot, appeared on the JumboTron. The Georgia cheerleaders and band followed, igniting the growing crowd's enthusiasm with each passing moment.

At 7:45 p.m., the stadium ceremony began in earnest. The strategic dimming of lights created anticipation as the JumboTron filled with Georgia red, reinforcing that this was indeed Saturday in Athens. The tunnel beneath the jumbotron began filling with red smoke, backlit by bright lights for dramatic effect and red fireworks from the top of the stadium. Three large *G* flags carried by cheerleaders emerged from the smoke, followed by the Georgia football team, sending the crowd into a frenzy. In perfect contrast, the Tennessee Volunteers' entrance from the opposite end zone was met with a thunderous chorus of boos, completing the electric atmosphere of this SEC showdown.

The first half proved to be the competitive battle everyone expected between these two SEC powerhouses. As the teams traded blows, the packed stadium swayed between nervous tension and explosive celebration with each momentum shift. Both squads demonstrated why they were highly ranked, matching each other's intensity drive for drive. When the teams headed to their locker rooms at halftime, the 17–17 deadlock perfectly reflected the evening's competitive balance, leaving fans from both sides anxiously anticipating the second half.

The final two quarters, however, told a completely different story. Georgia emerged from the break, asserting their dominance on both sides of the ball. The Bulldogs' offense found another gear, putting up fourteen unanswered points that would prove to be the difference in the game. Meanwhile, their defense clamped down on Tennessee's previously effective attack, shutting out the Volunteers in the second half. The final score of 31–17 reflected Georgia's superior adjustments and execution after halftime, sending the home crowd into celebration.

As the game clock wound down and victory was secured, the famous hedges witnessed another Georgia triumph between them. The experience had delivered everything I'd hoped for and more—from the early morning GameDay excitement to the evening's dramatic conclusion. Every moment of this Saturday in Athens reinforced why college football holds such a special place in American sports culture.

Every element of the pregame experience—from my personal moment with the hedges to the orchestrated team entrances—demonstrated why Georgia football in Sanford Stadium holds such a special place in college football lore. The traditions, pageantry, and raw energy combined to create an unforgettable prelude to the game itself.

As the final seconds ticked off the clock and fans began their exodus, I remained in my seat, taking in the emptying stadium while allowing the traffic to clear. For thirty minutes, I watched the cleaning crew begin their work and enjoyed the peaceful comedown from the game's intensity. Before leaving, I spotted and collected an abandoned Georgia Bulldogs souvenir cup: a small but meaningful memento from this memorable evening.

The thirty-minute walk back to my car under the Athens night sky provided time for reflection. The stadium lights still illuminated the darkness behind me as I retraced my steps through campus, now quiet except for distant celebrations and the occasional passing group of happy Bulldog fans. Each step brought back memories from different moments of this rich day: the morning GameDay excitement, Sims' welcoming tailgate, the taste of John's beef on wick, my reunion with Roger, and the countless conversations with passionate fans.

During the two-hour drive back to Atlanta, I found myself thinking about how college football creates these unique spaces where people from all walks of life come together. In a country often divided by various issues, none of those potentially conflicting topics ever surfaced. Instead, the day was filled with discussions about traditions, team loyalties, shared experiences, and the simple joy of college football. The sport provided common ground where differences dissolved into a shared passion for the game and its traditions.

The venue had lived up to its historic reputation, from the iconic hedges to the electric atmosphere. The food had told the story of Southern hospitality, while the people I'd met— whether brief encounters or longer conversations—had added their own chapters to this week's tale. Steven's parallel bucket list dreams, Sims's generous hospitality, and Roger's warm reunion all contributed to making Week Twelve special.

As my wife and I traveled back to Austin the following day, I found myself reflecting on the extraordinary experiences of the past weeks. Each stop had brought its own flavor to my journey, building a tapestry of American college football culture. Despite the mounting weeks behind me, my enthusiasm hadn't faded. Instead, I felt energized and eager for Week Thirteen's upcoming adventure in Norman to see the Alabama Crimson Tide take on the Oklahoma Sooners. The countdown to next weekend had already begun in my mind, as this journey continued to exceed my expectations with each passing week.

#7 ALABAMA AT OKLAHOMA

The planning for Week Thirteen began back in late July and early August when I was mapping out potential games for my bucket list journey. Several matchups caught my attention: NC State versus Georgia Tech with a chance to visit Atlanta, along with possibilities of Indiana at Ohio State, and Arizona at TCU. However, having already experienced TCU and Ohio State earlier in the season and Georgia the previous week, one game particularly stood out: Alabama at Oklahoma. This promised to be an intriguing late-season SEC matchup. The anticipation of this showdown led me to book my airfare, secure an Airbnb, and purchase my game ticket on August 12th. As the season unfolded and Week Thirteen approached, the dynamics had shifted considerably. Alabama was ranked number 7, while Oklahoma remained unranked and was fighting just to achieve bowl eligibility. As a Texas alum with no particular allegiance to either team (in fact, a subtle dislike of both), I decided on a neutral approach to my gameday attire. I chose a gray hat and maroon hoodie that would allow me to blend seamlessly with both teams' fan bases, since maroon was a shared color between them.

I touched down in Oklahoma City late morning on Friday, November 22nd, eager to explore a city I had never visited before. My initial plans faced a slight scheduling challenge:the Airbnb wouldn't be available for check-in until after 3 p.m., and my former classmate Adiaha, who had made Oklahoma City her home, couldn't meet until after 4 p.m.. With several hours to fill and finding myself in a city rich with history, my thoughts turned to a significant historical event that had shaped not just Oklahoma City, but the entire nation. I remembered the Oklahoma City bombing from 1995 and wondered if there might be a memorial site. A quick Google search confirmed there was indeed a memorial on the very grounds where the tragedy had occurred. The memorial was conveniently located about twenty minutes from the airport and fifteen minutes from my Airbnb, making it the perfect way to meaningfully spend my free hours before my later commitments.

The Oklahoma City National Memorial stands as a testament to one of America's darkest moments: a domestic terrorist attack that claimed 168 lives and injured hundreds more on April 19, 1995. Being twenty-three years old when the bombing occurred, I had vivid memories of how the events unfolded, particularly the connection to the Branch Davidian incident in Waco, Texas, two years prior. The bomber had been deeply influenced by what he perceived as government overreach in the Waco situation, ultimately choosing to strike on its anniversary.

The memorial's design proved to be powerfully moving and masterfully executed. As I entered the grounds, I was immediately struck by the symbolic elements that greeted visitors. The 9:01 Gate marked the moment before the city and nation were forever changed. The Survivor's Wall, bearing the names of those who lived through the attack, stood as a testament to resilience. Perhaps most poignant was the Field of Empty Chairs: 168 bronze and glass chairs, arranged in nine rows representing each floor of the building, with smaller chairs representing the children lost that day. These chairs, illuminated from beneath, faced a serene reflecting pool that stretched between the 9:01 and 9:03 Gates, marking the moment before and after the bombing.

During my two-and-a-half hour visit, the museum's chronological presentation helped me connect my personal memories with the fuller historical narrative. Each exhibit thoughtfully detailed the events of that day—from the normal morning routines that were violently interrupted to the chaos and heroism that followed. The museum housed striking artifacts: twisted pieces of the building, personal items recovered from the site, and detailed accounts from survivors and first responders. One particularly moving exhibit featured actual audio recordings from that morning's water resources board meeting that captured the explosion.

What struck me most was how the memorial balanced the gravity of the tragedy with a message of hope and resilience. The Survivor Tree, an American elm that withstood the blast, stood as a living symbol of survival. The Children's Area, filled with messages and drawings from young people across the country, reminded visitors that even in our darkest moments, hope prevails. As I concluded my visit, I found myself deeply moved by how this memorial not only honored those lost but also celebrated the strength of a community that refused to be defined by tragedy. The experience left me with a heightened appreciation for how the city had transformed a site of unimaginable horror into a place of remembrance, reflection, and healing.

This senseless act of domestic terrorism not only changed a city and nation forever but created a sacred space where future generations will come to learn, reflect, and grapple with humanity's capacity for both devastating hatred and remarkable healing. The Oklahoma City National Memorial stands not just as a monument to those lost, but as an eternal echo of that haunting question that no exhibition, no artifact, and no explanation can fully answer. Why? It's a question that will resonate through time, challenging each new generation to confront the consequences of extremism while embracing the hope and resilience that emerged from that dark April morning.

After departing the memorial, emotionally moved by the experience, I headed to my Airbnb to check in and decompress for a brief moment. Around 4 p.m., I met up with my former classmate Adiaha at a local gem called The Kitchen, a soul food restaurant that lived up to its reputation. The meal proved to be exactly what I needed: their catfish was perfectly crispy, the fries were seasoned just right, and I even treated myself to some homemade pound cake to take back for a late-night snack. Adiaha and I spent a couple of hours catching up on family, friends, and reminiscing about old times, providing a warm and welcomed contrast to the solemnity of my morning visit to the memorial.

With Saturday's game scheduled for a 6:30 p.m. kickoff, I had the luxury of taking it easy Friday evening. I returned to my Airbnb, watched some football, and settled in for a relaxing night, knowing I wanted to get an early start the next day to fully experience game day in Norman. The day had perfectly balanced meaningful reflection with casual reconnection, setting the stage for the football excitement to come.

Saturday morning arrived with the anticipation of game day in Norman. After a good night's rest, I got dressed in my neutral-colored

attire and recorded my weekly video update. Hungry for a local breakfast experience, I made my way to Neighborhood Jam, a wonderful
spot that proved to be the perfect start to my game day. After enjoying a satisfying breakfast, I pointed my GPS toward Norman, about
thirty minutes away from Oklahoma City. I arrived on campus just
shy of 11 a.m., following the navigation system's directions to Oklahoma Memorial Stadium. In what had become a consistent pattern
during my football travels, I drove as close to the stadium as possible until I found convenient street parking. Here, I found a spot
along Hoover Street, just off the main thoroughfare of Lindsay Avenue. I stumbled upon it by chance: free parking within walking distance of both the stadium and campus. From there, I made my way
up Elm Avenue, ready to immerse myself in the University of Oklahoma's gameday atmosphere.

As I made my first steps onto the University of Oklahoma campus, I was immediately struck by its pristine presentation. With a
student population of 34,000, the grounds were meticulously maintained, with expansive lawns that created an open, welcoming atmosphere. The architectural character of the well-established buildings
spoke to the university's rich history, while their maintained con-
dition reflected a clear pride in the institution. What particularly
caught my attention—and would become one of my most memorable observations—were the distinctive red telephone booths scattered throughout campus. These weren't just decorative remnants of
a bygone era but were actually functioning phones, a charming and
unique feature I hadn't encountered on any other campus visits: and
it was these small, seemingly insignificant things that I appreciated
about each campus I visited. As I wandered the grounds, I captured
photos of the striking bell tower and found myself appreciating how

the campus seamlessly blended traditional collegiate architecture with modern amenities.

The campus had a natural flow to it, leading me past various administrative buildings, residence halls, and academic centers. My path eventually brought me to the student union, which, like many of my previous campus visits, served as a central hub of activity. However, this one distinctly embraced its "Sooner" identity throughout. Of particular interest was the impressive replica of the covered wagon the Sooner Schooner: a white wagon featuring its name in bold red lettering and matching red wheels. I took time to read about the Roughnecks, the dedicated group responsible for preserving this important piece of Oklahoma tradition. Like other university unions I'd visited, this one offered plenty of spaces for people-watching, various dining options, and student services, but with that unmistakable Oklahoma spirit woven into every aspect of the facility.

As the afternoon began to unfold, I made my way to what locals called "Campus Corner": a vibrant hub of gameday activity situated at the intersection of Asp Street and Boyd. This wasn't your typical tailgating scene with rows of tents and parking-lot parties. Instead, it was a dynamic street festival atmosphere where brick-and-mortar establishments merged with the energy of gameday. The area was alive with a mix of restaurants, bars, shops, and street vendors, naturally guiding fans as they drifted from one spot to another or settled into their go-to hangouts.

During my exploration, I struck up a conversation with Jason, a friendly local who was there with his family. When I shared my story about the fourteen-week tailgate bucket list journey, Jason was intrigued and responded, "Bro, that's awesome—I'd love to do something like that one day." That is, until I mentioned I was from Austin.

His playful response of giving me the "horns down" gesture would turn out to be a recurring theme throughout the day, an interesting cultural quirk that seemed deeply embedded in Oklahoma's football identity, even when they weren't playing Texas. This interaction was my first glimpse into the deep-seated rivalry that apparently never takes a week off.

At 2:45 p.m., my phone lit up with a text message that would shift my usual gameday routine. Another classmate of mine, Kevin, who lived in Dallas, happened to be in Norman with his wife, Missy, and brother and sister-in-law for a separate event. They were posted up at Coach's Corner, a bar coincidentally located near where I had parked earlier that morning. I decided to deviate from my typical tailgating approach and make the roughly thirty-minute walk back to join them. When I arrived, I found Kevin, Missy, Dante, and Pam in high spirits. The latter two, being Oklahoma alumni, shared fascinating insights about the university's history and traditions, while also showing sincere interest in hearing about my previous games and my impressions of their campus.

We settled in for some wings while catching other college games on the bar's TVs, creating our own little gameday sanctuary. The atmosphere at Coach's Corner was particularly welcoming, especially when the owner, Corey, personally came over to introduce himself. He was fascinated by my bucket list journey, and we enjoyed a great conversation about college football and what brought me to Norman. This impromptu gathering turned into one of those unexpected highlights that make these trips special—where planned events give way to organic moments of connection and community.

Around 4:30 p.m., with kickoff a couple of hours away, I bid farewell to Kevin and the group, knowing I had a solid thirty-minute walk back toward the stadium. As I made my way through campus, the late afternoon air carried the enticing aroma of barbecue and the sound of music growing louder with each step. Following these sensory cues, I discovered a lively tailgate scene near the Jefferson Garage, hosted by the Black alumni group. There, I met Brandon from Houston, who greeted me with "Boomer Sooner"—the rally cry of Oklahoma fans that echoes their pride and tradition, who was enjoying the festivities with his family. After introducing myself and sharing my bucket list adventure, Brandon's enthusiasm for my story was infectious—so much so that he insisted I share it with his wife. Their response was classic Oklahoma: they welcomed me with warm smiles while playfully flashing the "horns down" hand gesture, which by now had become an amusing running theme of my visit.

The energy at this tailgate exemplified everything I loved about college football: the food, the music, the camaraderie, and the way complete strangers could become fast friends over a shared love of the game. This spontaneous stop proved to be yet another reminder of why I had undertaken this bucket list journey in the first place: these authentic, unscripted moments of connection that you can't plan for but somehow always seem to find.

Just over an hour before the 6:30 p.m. kickoff, I began making my way toward Oklahoma Memorial Stadium. Armed with my ticket for section 17, row 37, seat 27, I was particularly eager to witness one of college football's most storied traditions: the majestic Sooner Schooner, Oklahoma's horse-drawn wagon, thundering across the field. The anticipation of this moment had been building since I'd first selected this game months ago.

The migration toward the stadium felt like being part of a crimson tide (ironically, given the opponent), as 84,000 fans converged on this historic venue. Threading my way through the growing crowd, I located my section and climbed to my seat in the end zone, where I found myself next to an engaging gentleman named Jeff. He was attending the game solo, though his son was seated in another section. Our conversation flowed naturally as I shared my bucket list journey, and Jeff listened with keen interest. His connection to college athletics ran deep. He served on the board of trustees for a Texas university, and although he admitted to quietly pulling for Alabama because of his son's attendance there, he became an unexpected source of inspiration. In fact, Jeff suggested that my experiences would make for a compelling book or short story, a suggestion that would stick with me long after our chance encounter.

My end zone seats provided a sweeping panorama of the stadium, offering a perfect view of the pregame festivities unfolding below. The Pride of Oklahoma marching band commanded the field, their formations precise and deliberate as they spelled out "OU" while playing the fight song and the ubiquitous "Boomer Sooner." Above them, the massive JumboTron alternated between highlight reels and crowd shots, although I couldn't help but notice the curious continuing trend of fans giving the "horns down" gesture, a ritual that, again, seemed strangely disconnected from tonight's matchup with Alabama. This persistent rivalry hand sign, even in a non-Texas game, offered an interesting glimpse into the conditioned nature of Oklahoma's football culture.

The first half proved to be a display of Oklahoma's dominance, even if the scoreboard didn't fully reflect it. Despite controlling nearly every aspect of the game against the seventh-ranked Crimson Tide, the Sooners only held a modest 10–3 lead at halftime. During the break, I noticed something that caught my attention and, to be honest, rubbed me the wrong way. As the Alabama kicker came out to practice field goals, any ball that sailed over the protective net was caught by fans in the stands and then passed upward, row by row, until the last person hurled it completely out of the stadium. From what I could gather, this seemed to be one of those unwritten OU traditions—not that I have to like it. It is what it is. But as someone observing and documenting the culture of college football, I couldn't ignore how it didn't sit right with me. The behavior felt unnecessary, reminiscent of the bottle-throwing incident I'd witnessed at the Texas game earlier in my journey. Much like then, I felt the need to call it as I saw it, just as I had when fans from my own alma mater had crossed a line. Between this and the persistent "horns down" gestures—which felt oddly out of place at a game against Alabama—I found myself wrestling with certain elements of the gameday culture, even while appreciating the overall experience.

The second half unfolded as a continuation of Oklahoma's commanding performance, with the Sooners extending their lead to 24–3 through two additional touchdowns. The home team's dominance created a mounting sense of excitement throughout the stadium, building toward what would become one of the more memorable endings I'd witnessed during my bucket list journey.

With roughly two minutes remaining in the game, you could feel the anticipation rippling through the crowd. The impending victory over Alabama had the student section particularly energized, and what happened next was unprecedented in my gameday experiences. With twenty-eight seconds still remaining on the clock—before the game had officially ended—fans began storming the field in premature celebration. Stadium security, anticipating the possibility of goal post destruction, had already lowered them to prevent damage. The impromptu field rush created a surreal scene that forced officials to halt the game for a good five to seven minutes while security worked to clear the playing surface.

Once the field was finally cleared and the last twenty-eight seconds were played out, the inevitable Oklahoma victory triggered a second field-storming celebration—a rare "double" field rush that perfectly encapsulated the enthusiasm of the moment. The scene was electric, with thousands of fans blanketing the field in a sea of crimson and cream, celebrating their upset victory over the seventh-ranked Crimson Tide.

I remained in my seat for about thirty minutes after the final whistle, both to let the crowds thin out and to soak in the atmosphere. After collecting a left-behind OU souvenir cup—another addition to my growing collection—I began the half-hour walk back to my car, reflecting on yet another unique chapter in my football journey. This game had offered something I hadn't seen before: a double field-storming that spoke to the passion of Oklahoma's fan base and their jubilation at defeating a program of Alabama's stature along with improving OU's chance at being invited to a bowl game.

As Week Thirteen drew to a close and as I flew back home Sunday, I found myself reflecting on a weekend that perfectly embodied why I had undertaken this ambitious bucket list journey. From the passionate gameday traditions to the unique quirks of Oklahoma's football culture, every moment contributed to a deeper understanding of college football's diverse landscape.

This particular weekend stood apart from others because it encompassed so much more than just the game itself. My Friday visit to the Oklahoma City National Memorial had provided a profound and sobering counterpoint to Saturday's festivities. That powerful experience of remembrance and reflection set a tone of perspective that carried throughout the day. The opportunity to reconnect with my former classmates added layers of personal connection that made the trip even more meaningful.

The game itself had delivered its own memorable moments: from the iconic Sooner Schooner entrance to the unprecedented double field-storming that capped the evening. My conversations with fellow fans like Jeff, Brandon, and others throughout the day reinforced what I'd discovered throughout this journey: that college football serves as a unique catalyst for human connection, bringing together strangers through their shared love of the game. Week Thirteen had shown me yet another unique side of college football culture, adding another rich chapter to my growing collection of gameday memories.

On the drive home from the airport, the realization hit me that only one week remained in this extraordinary journey. Week Fourteen would mark not just another game, but the finale of a bucket list adventure that had taken me across the country, through countless stadiums, and into the heart of college football culture. With my final destination looming—and knowing I'd be closing it out in my home state of Texas—my mind was already racing with anticipation of how this remarkable chapter of my life would conclude.

CAL AT # 9 SMU

As the college football season reached its conclusion, Week Fourteen represented more than just another game: it marked the finale of my ambitious journey. From my earliest planning stages back in July, I knew this weekend would present unique challenges as it fell during Thanksgiving. Air travel during one of the busiest periods of the year seemed risky, and with some games scheduled for Friday, I had to consider the implications of leaving family celebrations early unless I brought everyone along.

The potential games for this final week included Georgia Tech versus Georgia, scheduled for Friday in Atlanta, and the renewed rivalry between Texas and Texas A&M in College Station. However, having already experienced Texas A&M in Week One, I turned my attention to options that would keep me in Texas with a drive to the game versus dealing with airport travel. Two games caught my eye: Kansas at Baylor and California versus SMU, both scheduled for Saturday. While the exact kickoff times weren't known during my July planning, both venues intrigued me. I had driven past McLane Stadium, Baylor's home field, numerous times as I traveled up I-35 but never attended a game there. Similarly, SMU's campus in Dallas was familiar from passing by, but I had never experienced a gameday atmosphere there.

I intentionally kept my options open, knowing the choice would likely be influenced by potential playoff implications or other factors that would emerge as the season progressed. As it turned out, both programs had interesting storylines developing. Baylor was having a solid 2024 season, though I had witnessed their overtime loss to Colorado in Week Four. Kansas, at 5–7, was struggling to maintain relevance. However, it was SMU that emerged as the more compelling choice. In their inaugural ACC season, the Mustangs had made significant waves, defeating ranked opponents including #22 Louisville in Week Six and #18 Pitt in Week Ten. Their impressive resume also included victories over Florida State, Duke, and BYU, establishing them as a potential Cinderella story in the first year of the twelve-team playoff format.

By Week Fourteen, SMU had climbed to #9 in the rankings and had already secured their spot in the ACC title game, with legitimate aspirations for a playoff berth. This unexpected success story made my decision clear. I would conclude my journey in Dallas, watching the Mustangs take on the California Golden Bears.

To prepare for my final game, I ordered a blue SMU hat online and reached out to my college roommate, Kevin, who lived in Dallas, to join me for the experience. With a 2:30 p.m. kickoff scheduled, I woke up early Saturday morning and dressed in a red V-neck sweater, blue jeans, and my new SMU hat. After recording my final pregame video at 6:30 a.m., I embarked on the three-hour drive to Dallas, where I picked up Kevin before we headed out together to SMU's campus. We managed to find street parking around 10:30 a.m., giving us plenty of time to check out the campus and nearby spots.

Kevin and I spent the early morning hours exploring SMU's meticulously maintained campus, which immediately struck us with its architectural consistency and attention to detail. Despite its relatively small enrollment of twelve thousand students, the campus projected an air of prestige befitting its status as a premier private institution. The overwhelming majority of buildings featured red brick construction with crisp white trim, creating a harmonious visual theme throughout the grounds. Mature oak trees lined the well-manicured lawns, their branches creating natural canopies over the walkways.

Our campus walk led us past an impressive array of facilities. We explored the outer edges of residence halls, where even the student housing maintained the sophisticated architectural standards of the main campus. The administration buildings and libraries stood as testament to the university's academic heritage, while the campus chapel added a spiritual dimension to the scholastic environment. The real beauty was in how seamlessly these different facilities blended together, creating an atmosphere that felt both intimate and expansive.

The intramural fields and athletic facilities, including the impressive basketball center and the historic Doak Walker Plaza, demonstrated SMU's commitment to both recreational and competitive sports. Given it was Thanksgiving weekend, most buildings were closed to visitors, including the student union. However, this didn't stop us from capturing a photo opportunity with the iconic SMU Pony Up sign displayed just inside the entrance.

As we walked, it became increasingly clear that SMU's campus was more than just a collection of buildings; it was a carefully curated environment where every structure, pathway, and green space contributed to an atmosphere of academic excellence and institutional prestige. The campus's location within the affluent Highland Park/

University Park area only enhanced this impression, with the surrounding neighborhood of magnificent homes providing a fitting frame for the university grounds.

Our wandering revealed the thoughtful planning that had gone into the campus layout. Despite its compact size, SMU managed to feel spacious and uncluttered, with each facility naturally flowing into the next. The physical manifestation of continued donor support was evident everywhere we looked. From the impeccable landscaping to the well-maintained buildings, everything spoke to a legacy of generous endowments and careful stewardship of resources. This was clearly a place designed to attract and nurture some of the world's brightest students, and the campus's physical environment played a crucial role in that mission.

The historical context of SMU's football program in the early 1980s added an interesting layer to our visit. During this period, SMU boasted an explosive backfield featuring future NFL stars Eric Dickerson and Craig James, earning the name "Pony Express" due to the school's mustang mascot and their lightning-fast running game.

However, the program's success was scarred by scandal. Widespread recruiting violations and improper benefits to players led to the NCAA imposing its harshest punishment ever in 1987— the so-called death penalty. This resulted in the cancellation of SMU's entire 1987 season and a series of crippling restrictions that followed, including the loss of dozens of scholarships, a two-year ban from bowl games and national television, and strict recruiting limitations. The fallout effectively dismantled one of college football's rising powers and left a legacy that still lingers today.

Since emerging from the shadow of the death penalty, the program had worked diligently to rebuild its reputation and establish itself as a competitive team. Their focus shifted to ethical recruitment practices and developing talent, aiming to once again attract skilled players from across Texas and beyond, but this time within the boundaries of NCAA regulations.

As we explored the campus that beautiful fall morning, with temperatures in the mid-50s and clear skies above, we noticed people already beginning to arrive despite being four hours before kickoff.

As Kevin and I explored the campus, we stumbled upon what would clearly become the day's epicenter of pregame festivities. A large digital screen commanded immediate attention, flanked by several elaborate tents with tallboy tables being methodically arranged. Even in these early morning hours, you could sense this space was being transformed into something special. The location, we would later learn, was situated along Bishop Boulevard, a distinctive street that carved an oval-shaped path through the heart of campus. The interior of this oval was rapidly coming to life as the setup taking place looked to be an expertly organized tailgate venue.

Something about the setup felt different from other tailgating experiences I'd encountered during my journey: this was more intimate and intentionally designed. There was an air of sophistication that aligned perfectly with SMU's aesthetic. Even though we were hours away from peak activity, the preparation underway suggested this would be one of the livelier spots on campus. Given SMU's compact size, we suspected this might be the primary tailgating location and made a mental note to return once the festivities were in full swing. This wasn't just another parking lot converted for gameday use; this was "The Boulevard"—though we didn't know its proper name yet—and it would prove to be the sophisticated heart of SMU's gameday experience, where tradition met celebration in a uniquely Dallas way.

By 11:15 a.m., having completed our campus tour, we returned to The Boulevard. This area was transforming before our eyes into the heart of SMU's gameday experience. The space was rapidly filling with an array of tailgate setups, creating a vibrant pregame atmosphere. Fans were busy arranging lawn chairs and erecting tents, while bounce houses for kids were being inflated, adding a family-friendly element. The air buzzed with anticipation as bands began setting up their equipment, promising live music to energize the crowd. Multiple TVs were strategically positioned, ensuring that early arrivals could catch pre-game coverage and other college football action from around the country.

Though we had arrived well ahead of kickoff, the growing crowd, the smelling of grilling food, and the sea of SMU red and blue colors all pointed to this area becoming the epicenter of the day's festivities. It was evident that The Boulevard was a crucial part of the SMU football tradition, where the community came together to share their passion and their support for the Mustangs.

The pride in SMU's impressive 10-1 season radiated throughout campus with an intensity that was impossible to miss. Fans and alumni arrived decked out in team gear, from pom-poms to SMU helmets, and even custom-wrapped trailers displaying Mustang pride. My first interaction was with Becky and Jeb, who warmly welcomed me and agreed to be part of my first video of the day. When I shared my fourteen-week bucket list story, their eyes lit up with interest. Jeb proudly proclaimed that his setup was "the best tailgate in the nation," and Becky insisted we return after noon when their setup would be complete, eager to prove their tailgating supremacy after hearing about my experiences at other schools.

As the clock approached noon, the area began filling with more people. Kevin reconnected with some familiar faces, Louisa and Garrett, and we spent time sharing my bucket list story, which continued to draw amazed responses and questions about my various gameday experiences throughout the season. Around 12:15, we returned to Becky and Jeb's tailgate, and they had truly delivered on their promise. Their spread included delicious fried chicken from Bubba's Fried Chicken, an impressive array of fruit, chips, cheese, and crackers, plus both alcoholic and non-alcoholic beverages. They explained this was their standard setup for every home game, though today's atmosphere carried extra excitement with SMU headed to the ACC title game and potentially the twelve-team playoff.

The Boulevard continued to buzz with energy as we met more people around Becky's tailgate, including Tammy, who was fascinated by my bucket list journey. Around 1:00 p.m., Kevin and I decided to make another lap around The Boulevard, promising to return to our hospitable hosts. We headed toward the northern end near Dallas Hall, where we found more open spaces and photo opportunities, including a chance for me to take a selfie with the SMU pony mascot, Peruna.

Despite SMU's predominantly white student population, we discovered a welcoming group of Black alumni and former football players who invited us to join their tailgate. We spent about fifteen minutes enjoying their hospitality, complete with hot dogs, burgers, and chips, while discussing the upcoming game. The atmosphere grew more electric as the SMU band marched down The Boulevard, energizing fans for kickoff.

The Boulevard had evolved into something more than just a typical college tailgate: it felt like an intimate neighborhood party. There was something natural and organic about how everyone came together in this particular section of campus, creating a unique blend of community and gameday excitement. Drawn back to Becky's spot by the outstanding hospitality we'd experienced earlier, Kevin and I returned, particularly intrigued by the gumbo being prepared by John and his wife Shirley.

My encounter with Shirley proved to be one of the most meaningful moments of not just the day, but perhaps my entire fourteen-week journey. We had returned to the area near Becky's tailgate, drawn back by Kevin's interest in some gumbo being prepared by John. As we approached, we met John's wife Shirley, and I shared my bucket list story with her as I had done with others throughout the day. However, Shirley's response was distinctly different. While she showed genuine amazement at my journey, there was a depth to her reaction that suggested she was processing it through a more profound personal lens.

As our conversation unfolded, Shirley shared a story that put everything into perspective. She gestured to her daughter, who was seated and present at the tailgate with a dog, and revealed that a few years earlier, her daughter had survived a traumatic dog mauling incident while pet-sitting. The weight of this revelation hung in the air for a moment, but what struck me most was not the tragedy itself, but how Shirley framed it within the context of living life fully. Despite the trauma their family had endured, here they were, choosing to embrace the joy of a beautiful fall day and the festive atmosphere of game day.

Shirley's perspective on life resonated deeply with me. She spoke about how the incident had fundamentally shifted her outlook, crystallizing her purpose around caring for her loved ones. It wasn't just about being protective; it was about ensuring her family could still experience life's pleasures while healing from their trauma. In that moment, our conversation transcended football and tailgating, touching on something more universal: the resilience of the human spirit and the importance of moving forward while honoring our experiences.

As Kevin and I continued our conversation with the family, I couldn't help but reflect on how life's journey contains these unexpected moments of connection and understanding. What started as a casual tailgate conversation had evolved into a powerful reminder that everyone we meet carries their own story, their own struggles, and their own triumphs. Shirley's openness in sharing her family's experience, and their collective determination to embrace joy despite past trauma, added a moving layer of meaning to my final weekend of this bucket list adventure.

As Kevin and I continued meeting people, including an enthusiastic fan named ZZ (yes, just the two Zs) who greeted us with an energetic "Go Ponies!," we couldn't help but appreciate how life's journey includes both triumphs and challenges. Around 1:45 p.m., the energy began shifting toward the upcoming game. We reflected on the incredible hospitality we'd experienced during our time on The Boulevard: the excellent food, drinks, and conversations, all enhanced by the perfect fall weather.

It was a pleasant ten- to fifteen-minute walk to Gerald Ford Stadium, a 32,000-seat facility that I described as a "split-level single tier stadium" with a layer of luxury boxes. The intimate setting perfectly matched the campus aesthetic, nestled within the beautiful neighborhood. My seat in section 224, row 1, seat 14, positioned me at the fifty-yard line on the Cal side of the field.

With the stadium about three-quarters full at kickoff, the pregame festivities began right at 2:30. The cheerleaders lined one end zone while stadium hype music played, and the SMU football team emerged through a dramatic display of fireworks and smoke. True to college football tradition, the Cal Bears' entrance was met with a chorus of boos from the home crowd. The game itself proved to be a showcase of SMU's dominance after each SMU touchdown, the cheerleaders would parade SMU flags across the field, followed by the live pony mascot galloping in celebration—a unique tradition that added to the game's charm. The ninth-ranked Mustangs over-whelmed the 6–5 Cal Bears, building a commanding 21–0 halftime lead before closing out with a decisive 38–6 victory.

As I made the drive back to Austin, my mind wasn't just processing the events at SMU, but reflecting on all fourteen weeks of my incred-ible journey. I thought about the wonderful people I'd met, includ-ing Shirley's inspiring story of resilience. The entire experience had delivered far more than I'd initially anticipated when planning this bucket list adventure. While I'd thoroughly enjoyed watching each game, I realized I hadn't focused on individual players or even spe-cific plays. Instead, I'd found myself immersed in the broader expe-rience: the magic of outdoor football, the culture of tailgating, and the simple joy of being present in these special environments.

This journey had provided a welcome respite from the nation's chal-lenges, allowing me to discover and appreciate life's simpler pleasures. Each weekend had offered its own unique culture and energy, creating a tapestry of experiences that went far beyond the games themselves. From the intimate setting of SMU to the massive stadiums of pow-erhouse programs, from early-season optimism to late-season play-off pushes, I'd witnessed the full spectrum of college football culture.

What started as a bucket list dream had evolved into something far more meaningful: a celebration of community, tradition, and the enduring spirit of college football. As I completed the final miles home, I was happy for having not just planned this ambitious undertaking but for seeing it through to completion. The games had been exciting, but it was the people, the stories, and the shared experiences that would stay with me forever, making these fourteen weeks an unforgettable chapter in my life.

ONE BUCKET DOWN,
WHAT'S NEXT?

A s I close the final chapter on my extraordinary fourteen-week bucket list journey through college football, I find myself reflecting on a season that made history in more ways than one. I had the privilege of witnessing the inaugural year of the expanded twelve-team playoff format, an innovation that transformed the landscape of collegiate athletics. During my travels, I managed to see six of these playoff contenders in action, including two memorable appearances by Ohio State, who would ultimately hoist the championship trophy. The raw emotion and electricity of college football was on full display, as three of my games concluded with thousands of euphoric fans storming the field in celebration: moments that epitomize why this sport holds such a special place in American culture. These spontaneous celebrations, where joy and tradition collide, served as perfect bookmarks to what would become an unforgettable adventure through the heart of college football.

Looking back, I was remarkably blessed with the weather

throughout this journey. Mother Nature seemed to smile upon my travels, providing ideal conditions that never disrupted my carefully orchestrated plans. Not a single flight was cancelled, no games were delayed, and the weather cooperated at every venue: a stroke of fortune that shouldn't be understated when planning fourteen consecutive weeks of travel during football season. My approach to planning proved to be the perfect blend of structure and spontaneity. While I meticulously mapped out each week's matchups to optimize travel logistics and accommodations, I intentionally left room for organic moments, particularly around tailgating and local exploration. This combination of careful planning and impromptu decision-making was a departure from my typically methodical nature, but it added an unexpected layer of joy to the experience. The flexibility to embrace the unexpected moments became one of the journey's greatest pleasures, teaching me that sometimes the best memories come from unscripted opportunities.

My decision to rent cars rather than rely on ride-sharing services proved to be crucial. By arriving early, I never struggled with parking, and I avoided the postgame chaos of waiting for rides. Additionally, some venues were quite distant from my accommodations, making personal transportation essential. The physical demands of attending these games—the extensive walking and standing—were significant but manageable aspects of the experience.

Throughout my journey, several experiences stood out as truly exceptional, earning their place on my personal "best of" list. The title for most impressive fan base unquestionably belongs to Texas A&M. Despite my allegiance to the Longhorns, I couldn't help but be captivated by the Aggies' "12th man" tradition—a cultural phenomenon that I believe stands unmatched in college football. Their unified spirit and unwavering dedication created an atmosphere that has to be experienced to be truly appreciated. The Big House at Michigan fulfilled a long-held dream and earned its place as my favorite stadium. Its sheer magnitude, distinctive blue and yellow color scheme, and unique center-field tunnel—a departure from the traditional end-zone placement—created an architectural masterpiece that lived up to years of anticipation. When it comes to the most spectacular single moment, the nighttime drone show at Texas was nothing short of magical, creating a mesmerizing display that transformed the night sky into a canvas of light and motion. In the category of band performances, I had to create two distinct classifications due to the vastly different styles and traditions. Among the PWI (Predominantly White Institutions), Ohio State's band claimed top honors with their masterful Frank Sinatra-themed halftime show and the iconic Script Ohio formation: a spectacle I'd seen countless times on television but proved even more impressive in person. The HBCU category was defined by the extraordinary Fifth Quarter Battle of the Bands between Jackson State and University of Alabama Pine Bluff, introducing me to a rich tradition I'd never experienced before. This "game within the game" showcased the unique cultural heritage and musical excellence of both institutions. For overall weekend experience, Oregon emerged as the clear winner, offering a perfect trifecta of exceptional hospitality, a remarkable venue, and the breathtaking backdrop of autumn foliage that transformed the entire experience into something truly magical.

Now to the Yes/No portion of this book. No, this bucket list wasn't an end-of-life decision. Did I get what I wanted out of this journey? Yes. Was this expensive? Yes, but it didn't take me to zero. Knowing what I know now would I do it all over again? Absolutely! Would I change anything about the planning, venues, or details of any of the fourteen weeks? Not a thing.

Throughout this journey, I meticulously documented every moment, amassing an impressive collection of 806 photographs and 379 videos. While I'm not one for social media, I created a more intimate way of sharing my experiences. It began in Week One, when I attended my first game with DKirk, Greg, and Mitch. That initial shared experience spawned a dedicated text thread that would become a weekly tradition. I found that by keeping them engaged with regular updates, photos, and videos, they became invested participants in my journey, eagerly anticipating each week's dispatches about the unique traditions, tailgating scenes, stadium atmospheres, and local cuisine. Their curiosity was infectious, leading to engaging conversations about every aspect of each venue.

Similarly, I maintained consistent communication with my family, sharing nearly every capture with my wife and daughters. The experience took on new meaning as I became a sort of cultural correspondent, fielding questions about everything from fan behavior to food options, stadium logistics to local traditions. I methodically organized all media by week on my computer, creating fourteen distinct folders that chronicled each step of the adventure. This systematic documentation not only preserved the memories but proved invaluable during the writing of this book. What began as personal record-keeping evolved into a shared experience, with family and friends becoming remote participants in my journey. They witnessed my growth as I stepped out of my comfort zone, approaching strangers and immersing myself in new environments. Their questions were consistent: "How did people receive you?" "What was the culture like?" "What did you eat and drink?" "Tell us about the fan base!"

This virtual inclusion of my loved ones added an unexpected layer of richness to the experience, transforming what could have been a solitary adventure into a shared journey of discovery.

Reflecting deeply on the concept of a bucket list, I've come to realize something rather striking: I've never personally encountered anyone who has undertaken such a deliberate and structured journey of fulfillment. The very notion of a bucket list, I've discovered, isn't about facing mortality as many might assume. Instead, it's about confronting those persistent whispers of "someday" that we all carry within us. It's those experiences we've filed away with tentative phrases like "I'm thinking about," "I wish," "I might," "I want," or those three particularly haunting words: *coulda, woulda, shoulda.* These phrases are often the signposts pointing toward our unfulfilled desires, the adventures we've postponed for that elusive "perfect time."

Through my interactions during tailgates, game days, and casual conversations about my journey, I've discovered that while most people find the idea of a bucket list inspiring, very few take the leap to pursue one. But here's what I want to emphasize: don't force it. Your bucket list item should resonate naturally, striking a chord deep within you that simply won't be silenced. When you recognize that genuine desire, you'll know it with absolute certainty. Yes, the journey may present challenges, but nothing worthwhile comes without them. The key is taking that first decisive step.

I'm not planning to replicate this exact experience—nor should I. It was perfect as it was, providing exactly the rich, transformative experience I sought. While I might attend a few games annually or explore different HBCU homecomings each year, trying to re-create this structured adventure would somehow diminish its uniqueness. This journey wasn't about checking boxes; it was about embracing a long-held passion in a way that pushed me beyond my comfort zone while remaining true to my authentic interests.

To those reading this book, consider this your permission slip to pursue your own dreams. You don't need to structure it exactly as I did—your bucket list should be as unique as you are. The essential thing is to recognize what truly calls to you and then, most importantly, to act on it. Be Mr. or Mrs. Do; leave behind the realm of "someday" and step boldly into "today." After all, the most memorable journeys often begin with a single decision to stop waiting and start doing.

When I reflect back on my "why" for this journey, it all centered on my passion for college football. I wanted to create an experience that would allow me to explore the rich diversity of the sport in all its forms. This meant visiting new venues, witnessing both HBCU and PWI programs, and immersing myself in the various stadium atmospheres, food scenes, and cultural traditions that make college football so unique. The fourteen-week timeframe proved to be perfect, maintaining my enthusiasm and excitement throughout the entire journey. What I discovered was that each week brought dual joy: the satisfaction of processing the experience I'd just had, coupled with the anticipation of the upcoming weekend's unknown adventures. But perhaps the most profound discovery was how football serves as a powerful unifier, bringing together people from all different walks of life on a Saturday for a few precious hours. During these games, personal circumstances, professional status, and even political differences seemed to fade into the background. People welcomed me with open arms, and I found myself deeply appreciating not just the games but the human connections most of all. While I certainly enjoyed the football, it was the people who truly made this experience special.

What started as a personal bucket list journey evolved into something far more meaningful: I found myself both inspiring others and being inspired by the stories of those I met along the way. This beautiful byproduct wasn't part of my original plan, but it became one of the most valuable aspects of the entire experience.

As this extraordinary journey comes to a close, I'm filled with profound gratitude. First and foremost, I want to express my deepest appreciation to my wife, whose patience, support, and willingness to help sponsor this adventure made it all possible. She didn't just give me permission to pursue this dream; she actively encouraged it. I'm equally thankful for my daughters and friends who shared in some of these gameday experiences firsthand, as well as those who eagerly followed along virtually throughout the fourteen weeks, making each stop along the way feel like a shared adventure. Looking back, I'm confident in saying that this bucket list surpassed every expectation. Each of the fourteen weeks brought its own unique magic, from the largest stadiums to the smallest campuses, from traditional powerhouses to HBCU classics. I wouldn't change a single detail about any venue I visited or alter any plan I made. What started as a personal quest to experience college football in its many forms evolved into something far more meaningful: a journey that connected me with countless individuals, each sharing their own passion for the game and life itself.

The beauty of this experience lies not just in what I accomplished, but in how it might inspire others. Through sharing my story, I hope to encourage readers to identify and pursue their own dreams, whatever they might be. Remember, your *why* doesn't have to be the same as mine; it just needs to be authentic to you. The most important step is moving from thinking about it to doing it.

So as I close this chapter—both literally and figuratively—I leave you with the same encouragement I've shared throughout: don't wait for the perfect moment, create it. Don't just dream about it, do it. Your bucket list journey awaits, and I can assure you from experience, it's worth every step.

ABOUT THE AUTHOR

Often referred to as "Whitlock's Party of 4," Anthony, a proud husband and father from Houston, Texas, shares life with his wife and two daughters. He graduated from the University of Texas at Austin in 1994 and has remained in the Austin area, building a career in IT specializing in technical and sales roles. Known for his love of relaxation, Anthony enjoys chilling in the toes-up position while traveling to sandy beaches and blue-water destinations. He has a passion for sports, movies, and spending quality time with family and friends.

Anthony's inspiration to write stemmed largely from a desire to create a memento of his experiences for future Whitlock generations. He never aspired to write a book capturing his everyday life, but interactions with others on his journey who saw something special about the trips, which unexpectedly turned out to be more than just attending games, led him to give it a shot. He found the vivid memories that each week provided made storytelling easy to capture in words. Enjoy the book. And, remember, don't wait to move forward with your "someday" thoughts.

www.ingramcontent.com/pod-product-compliance
Lightning Source LLC
Chambersburg PA
CBHW071215090426
42736CB00014B/2838